New Idea
Dreams and you

JENNY MUNRO

Cartoons by Brian Kogler

Bay Books

About the author

Psychologist Jenny Munro is in private practice in Sydney, where she works extensively with dream interpretation and inner visioning as a path to healing.

She also writes a regular column for *New Idea* magazine, in which she interprets readers' dreams.

Dream interpretation has been a major theme in Jenny's work for over sixteen years since she first began exploring the inner world of the psyche.

Acknowledgements

My thanks to my parents, sisters and sons, who have so lovingly encouraged and supported my writing.

Special thanks to Upavas and to Margaret Munro, whose sharing contributed so profoundly to this book.

And to the thousands of dreamers who have shared their dreams with me.

This book is copyright. Apart from any fair dealing for the purpose of private study, research, criticism or review, as permitted under the Copyright Act, no part may be reproduced by any process without written permission. Enquiries should be addressed to the publishers.

Published by Bay Books, 61–69 Anzac Parade, Kensington, NSW 2033

Copyright text © Jenny Munro

National Library of Australia
Card number and ISBN 1 86256 384 5

Designed by Susan Kinealy

Typesetting by Savage Type Pty Ltd, Brisbane

Printed in Singapore by Toppan Printing Co

BB89

CONTENTS

HOW TO USE THIS BOOK   5

PART ONE   DREAMS AND YOU   7

1 — DREAMS — ALL ABOUT THEM   8
2 — DREAMS AND EVERYDAY LIFE   15
3 — DREAMS AND HOW TO INTERPRET THEM   27

PART TWO   THE LANGUAGE OF OUR DREAMS   37

DREAM SYMBOLS AND THEIR MEANINGS   38

Accidents 39   Aeroplanes 40   Animals 40   Antiques 45
Babies 91   Bicycles 46   Birds 46   Black 56   Blood 47
Boats 47   The Body 48   Blue 57   Bombs 51   Bride 80
Bridegroom 81   Bridges 52   Buildings 52   Bus 52   Cages 53
Camera 53   Cars 53   Catastrophes 54   Cats 41   Cemetery 54
Children 91   Circles 104   Circus 55   City 55   Climbing 55
Clothing 55   Colours 56   Cooking 69   Crescents 104
Cross 105   Crossroads 59   Death 60   Descending 61
Desert 62   Devil 62   Dogs 41   Earthquakes 64   Exams 64
Falling 64   Family 66   Fire 67   Fish 42   Floods 68
Flowers 68   Flying 68   Food & Cooking 69   Forests 70
Friends 89   Front/Back 88   Fruit 70   Gardens 70   Green 57
Hatred 71   Heatwave 111   Homosexuality 104   Horses 42
Houses 72   Illness 73   Incest 103   Insects 74   Ironing 75
Jewels & Jewellery 75   Journeys & Travelling 75   Key 76
Killing 76   Knife 77   Knock 77   Lakes 78   Laughter 78
Laundry 78   Lightning 111   Lost 79   Lover 93   Marriage 80
Mirrors 81   Money 82   Mud 83   Music 83   Nudity 83
Numbers 84   Obstacles 85   Oceans 86   Opposites 87   Out/
in 88   Paralysis 88   People 89   Pink 58   Photos 53
Places 98   Prisons 99   Prostitutes 99   Purple 58   Rain 112
Red 58   Religious Figures 94   Rivers 100   Roads 100
Rubbish 101   School 101   Seeds 102   Sex 102   Shapes 104
Shoes 105   Showers 105   Snakes 43   Snow 112   Soldiers 106
Space 106   Spiders 44   Spouse 93   Squares 105   Stars 105
Storms 112   Sunshine 111   Swimming 107   Telephone 107
Theatre 107   Toilet 108   Trains 109   Trees 109
Triangles 105   Twins 95   Up/Down 87   Victim 110
Volcanoes 110   War 110   Water 111   Weather 111   White 58
Wild Animals 44   Yellow 59

The author wishes to advise readers that dream analysis is a highly subjective matter. The interpretations given in this book should be regarded as a guide rather than definitive explanations of dream symbols.

Dreamers should always have the last word on the meaning of their own dreams rather than relying exclusively on someone else's analysis.

Jenny Munro

HOW TO USE THIS BOOK

All of us have four to five dreams a night, ranging in length from a few seconds to about half an hour. Over a lifetime, this adds up to around 100 000 dreams. A wealth of information and understanding is contained in all these dreams — about ourselves, our lives, our potential, our relationships and other people.

Freud once said that a dream not understood is like an unopened letter — a message from the subconscious mind that we have missed. Interpreting the whole 100 000 dreams would be a lifetime's work in itself, even if we could remember such a huge number of dreams — yet understanding just a fraction of them can provide us with enormous satisfaction and practical rewards. And, fortunately for us, if it's a very important message, then the subconscious will send us continual reminders in the form of a repetitive dream, so we have every opportunity to hear what it has to say.

This book is about getting the most out of our dreams — coming to understand ourselves, our feelings and deepest motivations; seeing others with the sharp and intuitive perceptions of the subconscious mind; and using dreams as a guide to the actions which will bring us greatest fulfilment and help us develop our strengths and potentials to the full.

Part One of the book is all about the nature of dreams and how they affect us. Chapter 1 answers questions about dreams such as why do we dream, and what happens if we don't. Chapter 2 looks at how we can use our understanding of dreams in everyday life: How can we stop nightmares? Can dreams be used for healing? What about children's dreams?

Chapter 3 is a step-by-step guide to interpreting our own dreams, and to using their guidance to enhance our waking life.

Part Two of the book provides in detail the meaning of many common dream symbols, and may offer clues to solving the mystery of baffling dream themes.

The language of dreams is a complex and often individual one. Sometimes none of the meanings given in Part Two will seem to fit your particular dream. If they don't make sense and you feel at a loss as to their significance, check back to the section in Chapter 3 on how to interpret your own symbols.

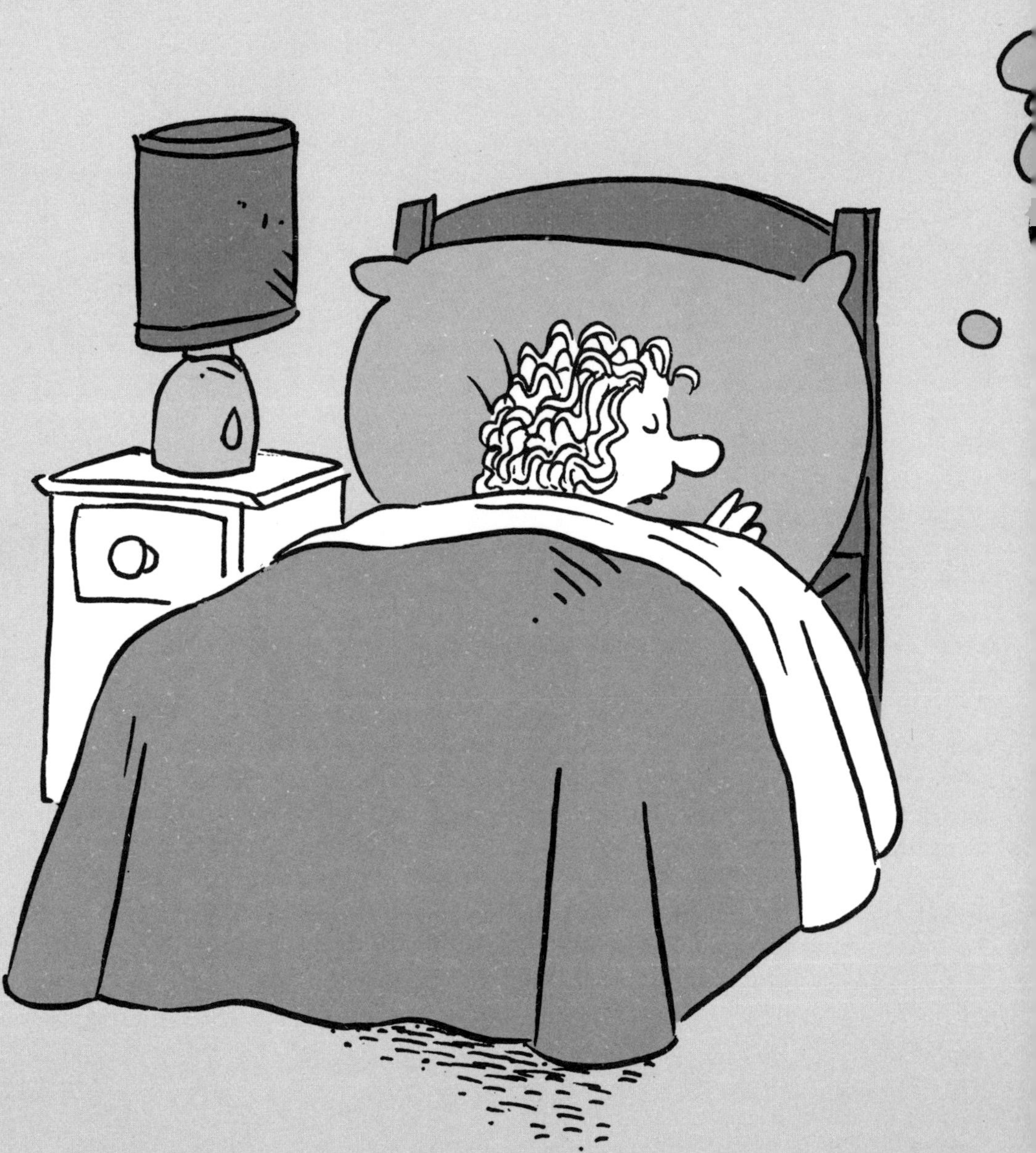

PART ONE

Dreams
AND YOU

What is a dream? Why do we dream? Do dreams foretell the future? This part of the book deals with these questions and many more about the nature of dreams and how they affect us.

Included is a step-by-step guide to interpreting and understanding dreams in positive ways which will enhance our everyday lives.

CHAPTER 1

Dreams
ALL ABOUT THEM

What is a dream?
A dream is that series of pictures and images, usually in the form of a story, that we experience while sleeping.

How do we know that dreams really mean something?
Dreams have been interpreted for thousands of years, and it's only in recent years that people have questioned their value. Some aca-

demic psychologists, for instance, believe that dreams are meaningless — that they are simply 'random electrical discharges' from the brain, or the mind's way of getting rid of its accumulated garbage from the day.

Of course, there is no way of proving objectively that dreams mean something. The way we conclude that they do have value and significance is by the results of interpreting them. If a dream can be interpreted in such a way that we learn something about ourselves, and that new knowledge improves the quality of our relationships, lifestyle or general wellbeing, then the dream has made an important contribution to the dreamer's life. Whether it can be 'scientifically' shown to 'mean' something becomes irrelevant.

If a dream helps us learn about ourselves it has made an important contribution to our lives.

The evidence is overwhelming that when people *do* pay attention to their dreams, by writing them down and attempting to understand them, their self-awareness and fulfilment in life increase substantially.

How long does a dream last?

The events depicted in a dream can seem subjectively to go on for hours or even days. However, research shows that most dreams actually last from a few seconds to a maximum of about forty minutes.

Most people, on waking from a dream, can give a reasonably accurate estimate of its length, regardless of how long it seemed while they were asleep.

Does everyone dream?

Yes. We all have four or five dreams per night. Some people will swear that they don't dream at all, but research has shown that in fact we all do.

Dreaming has been shown to take place during periods of rapid-eye-movement (REM) sleep. Observation of sleeping people reveals that for certain periods every night, our eyes move under the closed eyelids as if we were watching some inner story unfold.

When sleepers are awakened during REM sleep, they will almost invariably report having been dreaming, even if the content of the dream has been forgotten.

Dreaming, in fact, has been shown to be essential for mental health. If sleepers are awakened every time REM sleep begins — in other words, every time they begin to dream — and are thereby deprived of dreams, they will begin to show signs of serious emotional disturbance within a week or so. (Other sleepers awakened an equal number of times during non-REM sleep do not show the same disturbance.)

Dreaming has been shown to be essential for mental health.

So, not only do we dream every night, but these dreams, remembered or not, are vital for our mental and emotional wellbeing.

Why don't I remember my dreams?

People who have very full lives, perhaps with busy family, work and social commitments, seem to recall their dreams less than people who have, or make, time alone during the day for quiet reflection.

Similarly, people whose lives are undergoing changes such as moving house or changing jobs, or getting established in a new city, report that they remember fewer dreams than usual.

So dream recall seems to be a matter of attention. If our attention is exclusively on the activities of our day-to-day lives, and we have no reason to look within, then dream recall will be scant. Again, if our lives are going very well — if we are secure, well-adjusted and content — then we will tend to forget our dreams.

On the other hand, people who have good dream recall tend to be those who have a particular interest in the inner life, or those who feel that their outer lives could be more satisfying than they presently are.

How can I learn to remember my dreams?

Paying attention is the key to dream recall. If you want to remember your dreams, make preparations at night before going to sleep by putting pen and paper, and perhaps a torch, by your bedside. Go to sleep with the intention of remembering your dreams. As soon as you wake up, write down what you recall. It's important to do this immediately on waking. Many an interesting dream has been forgotten while the dreamer was making early-morning tea or having a shower.

Even if you recall only a fragment of a dream, or what you recall seems meaningless, write it down anyway. With time, more and more details of each night's store of dreams will come back to you.

Why do we dream?

There are many different opinions about the reason for dreaming. Some psychologists believe that dreams are simply the mind's way of releasing the trivia of the day; others that they are merely the mind's meaningless gibberish.

Dreams can illuminate problems and sometimes offer guidance for action.

Others believe that we dream to release tensions and explore conflicts about sexuality and power.

I believe that dreams are messages from the subconscious mind, drawing our attention to all kinds of considerations. Sometimes they reveal deep-seated conflicts that affect our daily lives, at other times they provide us with insights into our own motivation and feelings. They can illuminate the problems of our waking hours and sometimes offer guidance for action.

They can also provide a balance to our way of viewing a situation if it has become too one-sided.

I think that deep within us is a drive for self-development, self-knowledge and balance, and dreams are one expression of this drive.

IF SHE DOESN'T WAKE IN FIVE MINUTES, I'M LEAVING!

Why do I keep having the same dream?

The subconscious mind sends the same dream time after time when it has an important message to communicate and has not been understood by the waking self. It simply persists until the dreamer has responded in the appropriate way.

Sometimes a repetitive dream will stop apparently spontaneously. This occurs when we make the required changes without necessarily thinking of them as a response to the dream: perhaps we resolve our circumstances by changing jobs, speaking our mind in a relationship or taking a new attitude towards life. Since the situation has been dealt with, the dream is no longer required.

Almost everyone has repeated symbols in dreams. Over a period of a few months we might dream regularly of a particular place, person or thing. Again, this will cease when the message has been understood.

The subconscious mind sends the same dream time after time when it has an important message to communicate.

Sometimes a number of my dreams over a few months seem to be about the same thing. Is this common?

Dream series occur when the subconscious dreaming self is developing a theme, or reflecting our development in a particular area over a period of time.

Perhaps the dreamer is working towards a promotion. Initially, the dream may be of planning a mountain climbing expedition — the mountain representing the intended ascent to great heights. Later the dreamer might dream of going upstairs in a house with a winding, narrow and partly blocked staircase, the dream difficulties representing the real-life obstacles to promotion. Feeling insecure about being able to handle the job might lead to a dream of a falling lift. If unsuccessful, the dreamer might dream of being frustrated in attempts to find a way up to the top of a building. Success on the other hand might bring a dream of a wonderful view from a high place.

Common to all these dreams is the theme of ascent, making them recognisable as a dream series. (Ascent, of course, doesn't always refer to promotion, and promotion may be symbolised by something else, such as a new car.)

A dream series might also be recognised by a recurring symbol, such as a place or unusual detail. Reviewing the dreams of a series over a period of months can give us a fascinating summary of our progress, and is one of the rewards of keeping a dream journal.

What does it mean if I suddenly become aware that I'm dreaming?

Lucid dreaming is when we suddenly realise that we are dreaming.

Occasionally, in the middle of a dream, we suddenly realise that we are dreaming and that instead of being a passive member of the dream cast, we have a degree of autonomy. This is called lucid dreaming and is considered a very helpful means of personal and spiritual development.

So how do we make the best use of this awareness? Don Juan, an American Indian spiritual teacher in a series of books by Carlos Castaneda, advises looking at one's hands in the dream. This helps focus the attention and teaches us to see the 'essence' of things rather than merely their surface appearance. Other simple dream actions could be smelling a flower, or feeling the texture of a wall.

Lucid dreaming can bring much joy into our lives by expanding our awareness of other dimensions of our being, and increasing our sense of being able to direct our own lives.

Our ability to deal with nightmares can also be improved by lucid dreaming. Instead of fleeing from our dream monsters we can turn to face them, stand our ground with confidence and challenge them to explain themselves.

Is it possible to deliberately create a state of lucid dreaming?

It's difficult but possible. One writer has had good results by asking himself several times per day: Am I dreaming? After a while the question becomes a habit and is carried over into the dream state. The danger is that the habitual daytime answer of 'no' will be carried over into the dream state, too, so some objective criterion of waking or dreaming is required. He found that reading something twice is a good test. If we are awake then the words remain the same each time, whilst if we are dreaming the words will be difficult to read and will usually change.

Won't I get too introspective if I spend all this time on my dreams?

Our society is heavily biased towards the 'outer', everyday life, with its emphasis on achievement and material gain. Unlike some other cultures, we don't pay much attention to our inner processes, whether in the form of religion, meditation or the encouragement of self-awareness.

Our society is heavily biased towards the 'outer', everyday life.

So for some people, the turning inwards of attention that can come with intensive dream study can feel too introspective, particularly if they don't have other people to discuss their insights with, and their families dismiss or misunderstand their new interest.

Some people do become very inward looking for a time after beginning a quest for self-awareness, but this state rarely lasts a long time. And in any case, the dreams themselves will indicate if this is a problem!

As long as daily life is not disrupted by dream study, there's no danger of becoming too absorbed in it.

CHAPTER 2

Dreams
AND EVERYDAY LIFE

Do dreams foretell the future?
Popular folklore has always had it that dreams can foretell the future. Now and again they seem to do so, but the future they foretell is almost always to do with the internal state of the dreamer.

Perhaps we dream of moving house and a month or two later find we have changed our lives in some dramatic way. Perhaps we dream of a car accident and shortly afterwards fall ill. The seeds of these events will have already been present in the dreamer, at a deeply subconscious level, the dream giving us prior warning of their potential to occur.

Unfortunately it's very difficult to distinguish between warning dreams and dreams which refer to our present psychological state, or simply our fears. Dreaming that our spouse leaves us, for instance, or that a member of the family dies, is much more likely to be reflecting our fears of such a thing happening, than to be predicting the future.

It is extremely rare for our frightening dreams to come true.

It is extremely rare for our frightening dreams, or for that matter any dream about another person, to come true.

The main problem with this issue, of course, is that it's not possible to tell whether a dream is prophetic until after the event it predicted has occurred. This happens in only a tiny percentage of dreams. Usually the dream was highly symbolic and it was difficult to say exactly what it was predicting anyway, if anything.

So whilst dreams may on rare occasions foretell the future, it seems most useful to assume that they refer to the present, and interpret them in that light.

Having said all this, there do appear to be ways of assessing whether a particular dream is precognitive.

Denise Linn,[1] a writer on dreams, believes that there are three indications that a dream is predicting the future.

1. The dream is in colour, or the colour is unusually vivid.
2. The message comes through in three different ways during the dream. The message will appear in three separate, but distinct forms within one dream.
3. There will usually be a round or circular object within the dream. This can be an object like a ball or a round plate or a circular mirror, etc.

Remember that the dream will still need careful interpretation!

Why do I have nightmares?

All of us have nightmares at some point in our lives, and despite their varying content, they are always terrifying. Their purpose is to draw our attention to some deep-seated mental conflict, or fear, that has been too painful for us to face during our waking hours.

Insecurity and fears of failure, or of having our inadequacies exposed when we have been working hard to protect a positive image bring nightmares of falling or losing our clothes (see **Falling**, page 64 and **Clothing**, page 55).

Aspects of ourselves that we don't want to know about and pretend to ourselves don't exist (perhaps we think they are too aggressive or too sexy) can bring nightmares of being chased or having our house broken into. These disowned parts of ourselves gather strength in the subconscious mind and return to harrass us in our sleeping hours, often in the form of a monster, wild animal or menacing stranger (see **Wild Animals**, page 44 and **Unknown Man**, page 95).

[1] Denise Linn, *Pocketful of Dreams*, Triple Five Publishing, Sydney 1988.

Conflicting desires, particularly of a sexual kind, can bring nightmares of being unable to move. We may want and fear the same thing, and the result is a dream of being stuck, paralysed or fixed to the spot (see **Paralysis**, page 88).

Ignoring our needs for love and nurturing can bring nightmares of the illness or loss of a child. The child in the dream represents our vulnerability and need to protect and care for ourselves (see **Children**, page 91).

If we try to stifle a part of ourselves, such as aggressiveness or need for freedom, then we can dream of killing a person or animal, or watching them being killed. They represent the part of us that we are trying to kill off (see **Killing**, page 76).

Aspects of ourselves that we don't want to know about can bring nightmares.

Why can I go for years without having a nightmare, and then start having them again?

Our ability to handle stress and to deal with unpleasant truths about ourselves and our lives has a great deal to do with it. The more willing we are to consciously face and resolve our inner conflicts, fears and limitations, and the more confidence we have in our ability to take care of ourselves no matter what happens to us, the less likely we are to have nightmares.

Are children's dreams different from those of adults?

All dreams are symbolic, and can be interpreted using the same techniques — including children's dreams. Children's dreams, however, are often simpler. Perhaps because their ways of thinking and being have not become as crystallised and rigid as those of adults, their fears and conflicts are closer to the surface and not so heavily disguised in dreams.

For instance, a ten-year-old who was the eldest of three in a busy family, woke crying from this dream.

> I dreamed I was in a room full of luggage. There were so many bags, and they were all mine! I had to carry them round with me all the time.

This simple dream of heavy burdens and excess baggage indicated that the child was feeling burdened by the weight of responsibility she was being asked to carry in family life.

Many children have nightmares around the age of four, usually of being chased, or of having a witch or monster in the bedroom.

There are several possible causes. Firstly, the best and most loving

Many children have nightmares around the age of four.

of parents have a dark side to them: under stress they can become controlling, irrational and unpredictable. Because the child depends on adults entirely for love and survival, it can be frightening to see this dark side. Children may fear that this dark side of their parents poses a real threat to their wellbeing, so they may ignore or suppress this perception. Unfortunately, ignoring it doesn't make it go away. Instead it gathers strength in the subconscious and returns to haunt the child's dream, with the parent taking the form of a witch or monster.

It's not unusual for children to have these dreams, and does not in any way reflect on the quality of the parents' care. However, parents can ease the situation by noticing when they feel strung-out and snappy and discussing it with their children — explaining that everyone gets like this now and again, and reassuring the children that they are still loved and cared for.

Secondly, because the barrier between conscious and subconscious is thinner in children than in adults, children can be closer to their destructiveness. Everyone, adult and child alike, has an element of destructiveness in his or her makeup, but as adults, most of us have been largely conditioned out of acting on it. It shows up occasionally after the consumption of too much alcohol, or under extreme stress, but usually stays well-hidden in the subconscious.

For children, destructiveness is a stronger presence. Even if they are learning to handle it in their waking lives, children can become frightened by their capacity for extreme rage, and their capacity for murderous thoughts (both of which every child experiences). So as they learn to deal with these feelings in everyday life, their struggle can be reflected in nightmares where the frightening witch or monster represents their own frightening destructiveness.

Like all of us, children are more or less accountable for their actions, but not for their thoughts and feelings. It is our behaviour for which we are judged rather than our private ideas and emotions. Once children learn that they can have destructive impulses, but mostly control their destructive actions, then the nightmares cease.

Some psychologists believe that traditional fairy stories can help children cope with nightmares.

Some psychologists believe that traditional fairy stories can help children cope with the fears and nightmares of their early years. Such stories do not avoid destructiveness — on the contrary, they face it squarely and show that it can be mastered.

Fairy stories, myths and dreams all belong to the same realm of symbolic, psychological life, so reading fairy stories and fables to children can actually assist their development.

Another method which can be helpful for children experiencing nightmares is to have them draw their dream monsters. Crayons and paper have a way of bringing the most terrifying apparitions down to size in the reassuring light of day, especially if the child can then discuss the drawing with a sympathetic parent.

Should I help my children interpret their dreams?

I believe that only an expert should interpret someone else's dream — and even then, only offer suggestions, and only when asked. A dream is the dreamer's own property, and an interpretation coming from outside, particularly when unsolicited, is an invasion of privacy. It can be very tempting to look into a child's private world, yet we all need inner space to grow and develop without intrusion by others.

By all means take an interest in your children's dreams. This may take the form of listening to the child's dreams over breakfast without any comment other than 'That's interesting', or 'That must have been scary'. This encourages children to regard dreams as worthy of attention, so that as they grow they may start to interpret their dreams themselves if they want to.

Some dreams may have direct relevance to the child's parents and guide their actions, after consultation with the child. For example, the mother of the overburdened ten-year-old quoted earlier simply asked her daughter if she felt she had too much responsibility for her younger brother and sister and not enough time to herself. The child's reply was yes, and the parents rearranged their running of family life to allow their daughter to play, unimpeded by the need to supervise the other children. Their daughter was happier and more relaxed, and the dream did not recur. The mother didn't mention that she had been tipped off by the child's dream — it was not necessary.

What determines the content of dreams — is it only my psychological state?

I believe that most dreams have meaning related to our psychological state. However, there is evidence to suggest that physical conditions and the dreamer's health also influence dreams. Any kind of physiological stress appears to be reflected in dreams. Many people report, for instance, that certain foods give them nightmares. Anything from mushrooms to fish fingers, and eggs to wheat can trigger off a bad dream in individuals who may have a slight allergy to a particular food. Certain drugs can have a similar result.

Anything from mushrooms to fish fingers can trigger off a bad dream.

Perhaps the body's response to these allergenic substances is to trigger off a mild state of emergency or stress. This stress is communicated to the dreamer via a favourite nightmare: a warning to avoid the substance in future.

Anything that disturbs restful sleep, such as a high alcohol intake, will also affect dreams as they reflect the dreamer's physical condition.

Illness can sometimes be communicated to us in dreams before the symptoms have become apparent. Motor vehicles and houses are common symbols for the body, although they can refer to psychological states too.

And of course, being too hot or cold during the night can be mirrored in dreams of suffocation or bushfires on the one hand, and snow and frost on the other.

Vitamin B12 when taken in large doses at bedtime produces dreams in the most vivid colours. Take one milligram of B12 last thing before settling down to sleep for technicolour dreaming! Like other water-soluble vitamins, excess B12 is simply excreted from the body, so there are no dangers of side effects or overdosing.

Is it possible to choose the subject of my dreams?

Many people believe that they can programme themselves to dream on a particular topic, if they feel the need for insight or fresh understanding about it — or are just plain curious.

If you want to do this, make sure you have pen and paper by the bed, ready to record your dreams. Before you go to sleep, spend a few minutes focusing on your question and intending to dream about it. If this doesn't have the desired results, you could try the methods described under the heading 'Can dreams be used for healing?' on page 23, applying them to your particular area of interest.

Don't forget that because they are usually highly symbolic, the dreams might not initially look like an answer to your question. You might ask for a dream about a relationship, for instance, and find that the person doesn't even appear in the dream. Yet the dream might still be a response to your query: perhaps the person is there in a disguised form; the dream is describing your attitude to the relationship; or comparing it with previous similar relationships.

Do daydreams have the same meaning as dreams?

Daydreams are usually directed by our conscious minds so, unlike dreams, are not the symbolic products of the subconscious. However, it can be interesting to look at our daydreams and pay attention to what we're fantasising about.

The most common kind of daydream is the wish-fulfilment fantasy. We think of being with a particular lover, or imagine how it will be when we move to our 'dream' home, or when we get a much-desired job. We fantasise about being married, or being single, or being on a tropical island, or being rich, or having children.

Noting the details of our most common daydreams can help us plan the future — by putting money aside for a holiday for instance, or taking a course of study which will enhance our chances of promotion.

Spending some time daydreaming is natural and healthy. Doing too much of it, however, suggests that our lives are lacking something and that we are not taking responsibility for creating what we want, accepting the fantasy as a substitute.

Consciously directed fantasy can actually help us achieve our aims.

Consciously directed fantasy can actually help us achieve our aims. Imagining ourselves successful at sport, visualising every goal scored or winning tennis shot, seems to have a similar effect to physical training. Visualising a job interview and rehearsing in our minds possible questions and answers can act as a practice run. Seeing ourselves meeting a new friend and finding ways to talk easily and comfortably can help us communicate in social situations.

Does the menstrual cycle affect a woman's dreams?

Yes, it appears to for some women, particularly those whose menstrual cycle is synchronised with the phases of the moon, ovulating at the time of the full moon, and menstruating at the new moon.

During ovulation, a woman may have dreams containing symbols of the full moon, which traditionally represents fertility.

> I am giving opal earrings to my sister. There are several pairs in quite a range of colours and sizes. The pair that I'm particularly aware of contains large, round, pale, milky opals.

Anything pale and round like this in a dream can symbolise the full moon and therefore ovulation. Other symbols of the full moon include white animals such as horses, cats or rabbits.

Another common dream around the time of ovulation is that of giving birth, or holding a baby. Many women report that they recall more dreams around the full moon, and around ovulation, too.

Dreams occurring before menstruation have their own character. Frequently, they are more aggressive than at other times of the month, with scenes of violence in which the dreamer may be persecutor, victim or witness.

Dreaming of the colour red is common around the time of the period.

> In my dream I went downstairs to a cafe and met up with a group of girls, all of whom had red hair.

Going downstairs in this dream also suggests a woman's pelvic area.

> I dreamed I was in a courtyard paved with terracotta tiles in the most vivid red.

Occasionally, women dream of dead babies during menstruation.

Can dreams be used for healing?

Yes, dream interpretation can be used in the healing of physical and emotional problems, along with other suitable treatment, though it seems to require time and persistence.

There are several accounts of dreaming being used in this way: one woman's severe period pain was eased over the course of several months when she, together with her husband, analysed her dreams in great depth every morning. Another woman's great grief over the early death of her husband was considerably eased by the close study and understanding of the messages of her dreams.

It seems important to stimulate dreams on the subject, and there are several ways of doing this. One way is to spend twenty minutes writing on the subject before going to sleep. It doesn't matter what you write: the intention is not to be 'literary' but to pour your thoughts and feelings out on paper. When you have completed the writing, put the paper away without reading it, and don't look at it again for at least one month.

Another way to stimulate dreams is to draw a picture of the problem: what visual image does your illness, or your emotional distress or your present state of mind, conjure up? Spend ten to fifteen minutes drawing it before you go to sleep. I find pastels or crayons the

There are several accounts of dreaming being used in the healing of physical and emotional problems.

best for this. Remember, once again, that self-expression is the goal here, rather than artistic merit.

Either of these processes, undertaken every night for at least a month, will stimulate dreaming on the subject, so be sure to have pen and paper by your bed so you can write down your dreams, and be willing to spend time understanding them. If you don't understand a dream, don't worry; the meaning may well become clear within a month or two.

This method is not always easy, in that it requires persistence and can sometimes be frustrating when the meaning of the dreams seems impenetrable. The results, however, can be spectacular.

There's a lot of folklore about dreams — how do I know what to believe?

There is indeed a great deal of charming folklore on dreams, about everything from crystals to dream pillows. Here's a selection.

Dream Pillows

Dream pillows are small, handmade pillows stuffed with dried herbs. They are placed on one's regular pillow or close by where the herbs can be smelled and are said to enhance sleep and dreaming. Silk or wool are the best fabrics to use for the cover, and different herbs are said to have different effects:

Restful sleep: lavender and linden

Dreams: ash leaves, mugwort, artemesia; or camomile, mugwort or skullcap.

To prevent nightmares: camomile, rosemary, wood betony.

For prophetic dreams: mugwort.

Herb teas

Some of the herbs used to stuff your pillow can also be used to make a tea.

To promote dreaming: camomile, mugwort and skullcap.
To prevent nightmares: camomile, catnip, wood betony.

In the Middle Ages, it was believed that drinking a cup of mugwort tea before bed would allow one's whole future to be revealed in dreams.

These herbal teas should be made by steeping one or two teaspoonfuls of the dried herbs in a cup of boiling water for 5 minutes. Strain and drink a cupful of the tea before bed.

In the Middle Ages, people believed that a cup of mugwort tea before bed would help reveal the future in dreams.

Pearls

Pearls are said to promote dreams that help us intuitively understand a situation. Perhaps it's because they come from the sea, that symbol of the deepest layers of the unconscious mind. Sleeping with them under the pillow, or close by the bed, is said to result in 'pearls of wisdom' in your dreams.

Quartz crystals

These can be used for a number of ends in dreams. Because they are basically amplifiers and transmitters (a form of quartz is fundamental to the structure of computers) they are said to enhance one's purpose in dreaming, whether it is healing, understanding or foretelling the future.

According to tradition, to use a crystal for dreaming, first buy one which 'feels' right to you. Size and appearance are unimportant. Then cleanse it by washing thoroughly in cold water, leave it in sunshine for several hours, then in direct moonlight overnight.

Use it only for dreaming. Before going to sleep place it beside or underneath your pillow and decide what kind of dreams you want to have: restful and joyful; intuitive; healing. Be as specific as possible with your intentions for your dreams. Then imagine that your dreams are contained in seed form within the crystal, which will broadcast them to you in the best possible form while you sleep.

Amethyst, a type of quartz of a rich purple colour, is said to be particularly effective in promoting calm, restful sleep and preventing nightmares.

Quartz crystals are said to enhance one's purpose in dreaming.

Aligning Your Bed

Aligning your bed so that your head points towards magnetic north is said to not only bring restful sleep but also clearer dreams. Perhaps this is because the electromagnetic field of the body is aligned with that of the earth, bringing us into harmony with natural energies.

There can be no doubt that some of these methods do work for some people. Drinking herbal tea, for instance, has a physical effect on the body, so its results are to be expected.

But why do the other methods work? Perhaps they too have some subtle chemical or electromagnetic effect which directly influences us, receptive as we are in the dream state. Or perhaps it is simply the focusing of our attention on our dreams that is required for the use of these methods, that results in dreams of a particular kind.

Certainly they are harmless, they can be fun, and they can bring results. And remember: the dreams they bring will still need careful interpretation!

Are there any dreams which old people have before they die?

There are two kinds of dreams which are not uncommon for old people approaching the end of their lives.

The first is of passing through a gate. In young people, gates represent a transition of some kind, such as a promotion, change of lifestyle, marriage or the birth of a baby. The major transition of old age is, of course, dying. Often the dreamer will pass through the gate into a beautiful garden; occasionally the dream will contain religious imagery. Such dreams are almost always pleasant, and indicate the subconscious mind's lack of fear of death.

The other kind of dream about death is of a dazzling light.

> My husband died six months ago. Recently I dreamed I was in a forest and came to a clearing where a light shone so brightly that I could hardly look at it. My husband's voice said: 'Step into the light, Betty.' Part of me wanted to, but I was afraid, and I stayed where I was.

This dreamer has more living to do. Although part of her is ready to make the transition, she holds to life. The dream may also be telling us that, at a subconscious level, we have some influence over our time of dying.

CHAPTER 3

Dreams
AND HOW TO INTERPRET THEM

How do I go about interpreting a dream?
The first step in interpreting a dream is to write down everything you remember about it — the more details the better. Include the feelings you experienced during the dream (e.g. anxiety, guilt, anger, fear, distress, pleasure, excitement, indifference) and note down any thoughts or associations to the dream that come to mind on waking.

Dreams and you

The first step in interpreting a dream is to write down everything you remember about it.

> **Example**
> I live in a large, well-kept apartment with a big outside terrace. Peter (my eight-year-old son) and I are on the terrace. He is afraid of some dogs down below. I show him how to shut the gate at the top of the stairs that lead down from the terrace to the garden, but it won't stay shut. My friend, Margaret Sampson, comes to visit — because I am a single parent she has brought me a relief parcel containing lots of delicious teas and tins of food. I am very pleased.

Next, divide the dream into its different stages so that each one can be examined separately.

Next, divide the dream into its different stages or steps, so that each one can be examined separately.

> 1 I live in a large, well-kept apartment.
> 2 My son is afraid of the dogs down below.
> 3 The gate won't shut.
> 4 Margaret Sampson comes to visit.
> 5 She brings me a relief parcel because I am a single parent.

Each stage contains different elements and symbols, so we explore them one by one, by checking on their meaning in Part Two of this book, or reflecting on possible personal meanings.

1. I live in a large, well-kept apartment
Houses and dwelling places refer to the dreamer, so this dreamer is apparently taking care of her physical and emotional well-being and feels she has room to move in her life. The fact that she lives in an apartment and not a house in the dream, indicates perhaps her close interconnection with other people.

2. My son is afraid of dogs down below
The dreamer's son probably represents her own inner child (see **Children**, page 91). This inner child is afraid of dogs (see **Animals**, page 40) — perhaps representing the dreamer's own aggressive instincts, which come from 'down below', that is, from the subconscious. So this part of the dream indicates that the dreamer feels scared of her own aggressiveness or anger. She may fear that if she expresses these feelings, then there will be unpleasant consequences.

3. The gate won't shut
Try as she may, she is unable to 'close the gate' on her anger. Perhaps she fears that it will spill over into her everyday dealings in the

form of sharp words or criticism which are stronger than she consciously intends.

4. Margaret Sampson comes to visit
This was an old friend of the dreamer's whom she had not seen or thought of for some years. On reflection, she felt that this woman had appeared in the dream because of her surname, Sampson, (see **People**, page 89) suggesting great reserves of inner strength.

5. She brings a relief parcel to the dreamer because she is a single parent
This source of inner strength brings relief and nourishment — presumably emotional — to the dreamer in her role as single parent.

Having examined the stages in turn, look for any gaps in understanding of the dream as a whole. In this dream, for instance, what is the dreamer angry about? And why does she need relief from being a single parent?

As it happened the two questions were connected for this dreamer. She realised she was feeling angry about her responsibilities as sole caretaker of the children and needed occasional relief from them. She also saw that she was afraid that her anger and frustration would spill over into her relationship with the children.

This illustrates another point about dream symbols: that sometimes they can have more than one meaning. In this dream, the child, as well as representing the dreamer's own vulnerability and need for looking-after, also represents himself. The dreamer is afraid that the child will bear the brunt of 'the dogs below' — her subconscious anger.

The next step is to look for any solution that the dream offers to the conflict or problem it illustrates.

Interpreting the dream can give us useful insights into our own feelings and behaviour, but insight, on its own, is not always sufficient to help us grow and develop. Sometimes action is required, and reflection on the dream can give us a sense of what kind of action this is.

One writer on dreams calls this the 'dream task'. It can take a number of forms. Some of them involve changing our relationship to ourselves: does the dream indicate, for instance, that we need to look after ourselves better physically? The dream task might be reading about, and planning, an exercise, diet and relaxation programme. Or do we need to nourish ourselves emotionally? The dream task might be carefully reflecting on what we want and need for ourselves, such as time alone, a change of job, relationships where we are cared for, or an outlet for our creativity, and carrying that through. One woman's dream tasks were keeping her normally messy house clean and tidy, and taking up piano lessons!

Interpreting a dream can give us useful insights into our own feelings and behaviour.

Perhaps the dream indicates the need to take action in a relationship. The dream tasks might then be sharing feelings, asking for feedback, expressing needs and wants or setting limits on how much we are willing to do for, or take from, others.

Dreams can also provide guidance on how best to use our talents and energies.

An actress was having difficulty in disciplining herself to learn her lines and had the following dream.

> I was sleeping in a bed in the theatre. First thing in the morning, I was woken by a friend in the cast who asked me what I would like. I asked him for a cup of tea, which he then brought.

The friend in this dream was always very quick to learn his lines, and the dreamer recognised him as symbolising the part of herself which wanted to get on with the job. After some thought, she decided that the early morning was the time when this part of her was most active and decided to try learning her lines as soon as she had woken up and had a cup of tea. This method proved very successful.

Returning to our original example of the dreamer who needed relief from the responsibilities of single parenthood, we now look at possible dream tasks emerging from this dream.

Two main possibilities emerged: firstly, maintaining her inner strength through warm relationships and meditation; and secondly, arranging for the children to spend more time with their father at weekends. As she was on poor terms with him, the request required the strength of Sampson! She decided to do both, with very positive results.

The analysis given here is very detailed. Often the dreamer won't have the time or interest to go into every dream in this depth but doing so with the occasional dream can be very rewarding. And the basic procedure for dream interpretation remains the same even for a quick or superficial analysis.

Don't worry if you feel unable to understand a particular dream. Often the meaning will become clear some weeks or months later.

Sometimes dream symbols can be individual to the dreamer and initially very difficult to interpret. For example, I dreamed about New York on several occasions for a few months before I realised that for me, it referred to my new work. Sometimes the subconscious mind can be way ahead of our waking awareness!

And again, don't worry if your dream doesn't invite a dream task. Some dreams just need to be understood, with no requirement for follow-up action.

Sometimes the subconscious mind can be way ahead of our waking awareness.

Further tips on dream interpretation

Dreams love puns and word play! Often the images in the dream when translated into words, provide us with a familiar figure of speech which describes our present situation.

A dreamer who 'shoulders' many responsibilities might dream of carrying a heavy backpack. Another who subconsciously perceives a friend to be 'as mad as a hatter' might dream of an eccentric milliner. Another who feels 'bogged down' by domestic duties might dream of quicksand in the kitchen.

Often, writing down the dream in as much detail as possible will reveal the meaning of these metaphors — an example being the dream analysed in the previous section in which the dreamer received a 'relief' parcel. Any odd or unusual detail like this often holds a pun.

My dream symbol is not listed in Part Two, or the interpretation doesn't seem to fit my dream. How can I find out what it means?

Whilst some dream symbols, such as houses, or being chased, seem to have similar meanings for everybody, there are some symbols which are very unusual or particular to an individual which the dreamer will have to interpret. Or occasionally the usual meaning of a symbol won't make sense in the interpretation of a dream, and the dreamer will need to decipher it independently.

Here are some suggestions about interpreting symbols for yourself.

● Notice the feeling you had about the symbol in the dream — fear? curiosity? sadness? excitement? What is it in your life at the moment that provokes similar feelings? The symbol may represent that aspect of your life.
● Write down all your dreams for a few months. If a symbol recurs, look at the dreams in which it appears to see what they have in common.
● Write down all your associations to the dream, especially any you had when you woke from it — perhaps a song, a thought of someone, a word or phrase.
● Draw a picture of an aspect of the dream which is particularly mystifying, yet interesting. Then look at what you have drawn. Sometimes we can unconsciously express the meanings of symbols in the drawing, or the drawing might remind us of forgotten details of the dream which assist with interpretation.
● In your imagination, have a talk with the obscure symbol. In a relaxed state, with your eyes closed, picture the symbol in your mind and ask it: what do you represent? What are you doing in my dreams? Why are you behaving as you are? What do you have to say to me? Don't try to create replies in your mind — just let the symbol speak for itself and be open to whatever comes. Ask whatever questions you like, and use the method with any kind of symbol, from a water-tank to a funny hat, to your teacher from kindergarten. Sometimes no reply is forthcoming — yet the subconscious mind is often very happy to explain itself when directly asked in this way.
● Pretend you are telling an alien from another planet about your dream. The alien won't know what the objects you refer to in your dream actually are and you will have to describe them and explain their function or purpose. This can be enlightening for you. If for instance you dream of cotton wool and are explaining it to your imaginary alien, you might say: 'Cotton wool is soft white stuff that you can use to put in your ears when there's a lot of noise going on that you want to shut out.' This introduces a new dimension to the dream symbol: what noise in your life do you want to shut out — someone's complaints? Someone's continual demands? A high level of noise in your home when you want quiet?

Sometimes we can unconsciously express the meanings of dream symbols in a drawing.

Is the viewpoint of the dream always right?
No, it's not.

Firstly, dreams are almost always symbolic and not intended to be taken literally. For instance, we might dream of marrying a particular lover or taking a new job, but the dream is not necessarily giving us direct advice about the situation.

Instead, it may be referring to a deeper level of meaning where we develop in ourselves the characteristics represented by the dream lover — 'marrying' these qualities within ourselves rather than taking on a real-life partner — or the new job may symbolise a longing for variety or a fresh beginning in some other area of life.

Secondly, if we are one-sided in our view of a situation, a dream might exaggerate the other point of view to balance out our way of seeing it. The nightmares of unassertive people are an example: in waking life, if we find it hard to stand up for ourselves, then our dreams may be full of violent and aggressive action. The happy medium is a healthy assertiveness.

How do I know if I've interpreted a dream correctly?

Several things happen if we have truly understood a dream. Firstly, we learn something new about ourselves, or have something clarified, or see it in a new light.

Secondly, if we set ourselves a dream task and complete it to our satisfaction, a change takes place in us: we have more confidence, or more money, or a better relationship.

Thirdly, a correctly interpreted dream brings us a sense of recognition — a feeling of 'Yes, that's it!' — and satisfaction.

Do people need to interpret their dreams?

There are a number of paths to self-awareness, of which dream interpretation is just one.

Of course, not everyone is interested in self-understanding: many people are quite content with their lives as they are and feel no inclination to explore their inner selves or change in any way. Dream interpretation would be of no particular interest or value to them.

It can be of value to three kinds of people.

Firstly, people in crisis in their relationships or life generally, whether frustrated, depressed or simply dissatisfied, can gain insight into their experiences by understanding their dreams. This insight might then stimulate the action necessary to make a change — or be sufficient in itself to improve the situation.

Secondly, some people have an absorbing interest in understanding their own motives, feelings and impulses, and for them, dream interpretation can be a lifelong interest. Far from being a selfish pursuit, which this interest might appear to be on the surface, it enables individuals to increase their understanding and acceptance of others as they come to see that their own emotions, fears and passions are universally shared and are part of being human.

The third group for whom dream interpretation can be helpful are those who have an occasional vivid dream — perhaps recurring — which they feel has an important message for them. So rather than being a regular activity, dream interpretation for these people is an infrequent response to the need of the moment.

So dream interpretation is not for everyone. Other methods such as meditation, or various other spiritual pursuits, might be a more suitable path to self-awareness for some people.

But for those who enjoy their dreams and take a close interest in them, it can be an invaluable tool in self-understanding and development.

Dream interpretation is not for everyone. Other methods, such as meditation, might be more suitable paths to self-awareness for some.

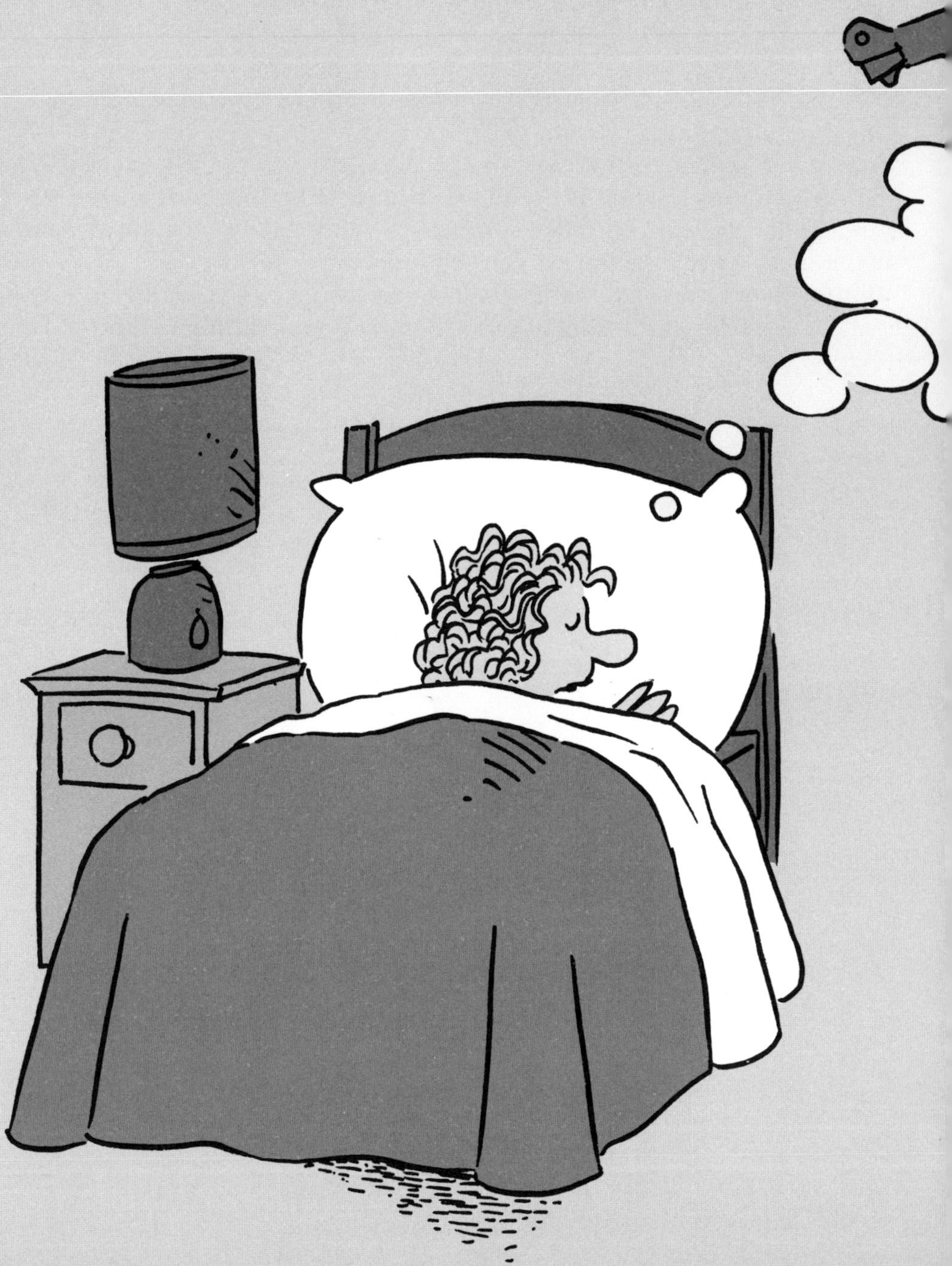

PART TWO

THE LANGUAGE OF
our Dreams

The language of our dreams is a complex and often individual one. Freud once said that a dream not understood is like an unopened letter — a message from the subconscious mind that we have missed. This part of the book offers a framework for understanding many common dream symbols and their personal significance.

Dream
SYMBOLS AND THEIR MEANINGS

Many of the dreams quoted are drawn from letters written to me for inclusion in my dream interpretation column in *New Idea* magazine. For that I am deeply grateful to my readers. The vast majority of letters I receive — around 97 per cent — are from women, and that is why I have used the pronouns she and her when referring to the dreamers in this book, more than he and him. The symbolism of dreaming, however, applies equally to men and women. Both sexes dream of similar symbols in similar ways and so the interpretations given apply to both.

I believe that I receive so many more letters from women than men not only because *New Idea* is a women's magazine, but because women generally (though not exclusively) seem to take a closer interest in their dreams.

Occasionally, the interpretation of a symbol differs depending on the sex of the dreamer, and I have made this distinction in the text where this occurs. Frequently in such areas, I have also used the terms 'masculine' and 'feminine' qualities. I believe that all of us have both feminine and masculine aspects and ideally we achieve a balance between the two in our everyday lives.

The 'masculine' qualities I consider to be the rational, practical and assertive. The 'feminine' qualities I consider to be the feeling, nurturing and intuitive. In our culture, the 'masculine' qualities have been overvalued and the 'feminine' undervalued — 'feminine intuition', for instance, has been treated with some suspicion and scorn rather than with the respect it deserves — and many people, both men and women, have developed their worldly, practical skills to the detriment of their subtle perceptions and understandings, and skill in human relationships.

In using these terms I want to emphasise that both sexes contain both elements and it is a natural part of human development for both sexes to develop both the masculine and feminine in themselves. In no way do I intend that women should be all feminine or men all masculine, or that one is better than the other.

I use these terms primarily in following the ideas of the famous psychologist C. G. Jung, and the tradition of Jungian writers, teachers and therapists who have had a profound influence on the understanding of dreams in this century.

ACCIDENTS

Accidents are the subconscious mind's way of saying 'slow down' or 'look after yourself more carefully' or 'make whatever changes are necessary at the moment'.

> I was in my car when I came to a bend in the road. As I approached it, I thought 'I should slow down or I won't make it'. But instead of slowing down, I put my foot on the accelerator, missed the turn and crashed into a tree.

A bend in the road usually refers to turning a corner in one's life.

A bend in the road usually refers to turning a corner in one's life — coming up to an important event or change. This dreamer knows he has to slow down to deal with what's coming up, perhaps by cutting back his social life or work load, but is speeding up instead

Collisions in dreams refer to confrontations. A head-on crash suggests a collision of values or views with another person.

— maybe to avoid looking at, or dealing with, the forthcoming change. The dream is showing him that if he doesn't slow down, then he simply won't be able to cope.

Collisions refer to confrontations. A head-on crash suggests a collision of values or views with another person. A near-miss indicates that the dreamer is narrowly avoiding conflict with someone else, and perhaps should have the argument out before a serious clash occurs.

AEROPLANES

Planes indicate rapid progress towards a goal without too much attention to detail on the way.

A frightening takeoff or landing may be suggesting that the dreamer needs to pay closer attention to details: that we will be more comfortable if we slow down and absorb them rather than rushing past them.

Aeroplane journeys can also indicate that the dreamer is ungrounded. Perhaps we are out of touch with the solid ground of reality, and have our head in the clouds. The details and emotions of the dream will provide further clues to its precise meaning.

Dream animals usually represent the instinctual side of our natures.

ANIMALS

Dream animals usually represent the instinctual side of our natures — our 'animal instincts', our primitive, natural aspects.

Cats

Women often dream about cats, especially if they have them as pets in real life. They may refer to the 'catty' side of one's nature, but more often to the mysterious, independent, feminine, magical aspect of a woman.

> My cat was very sick and I had to collect her from the vet. But I had to cross a very busy road and I just couldn't seem to get through the traffic to get to the surgery.

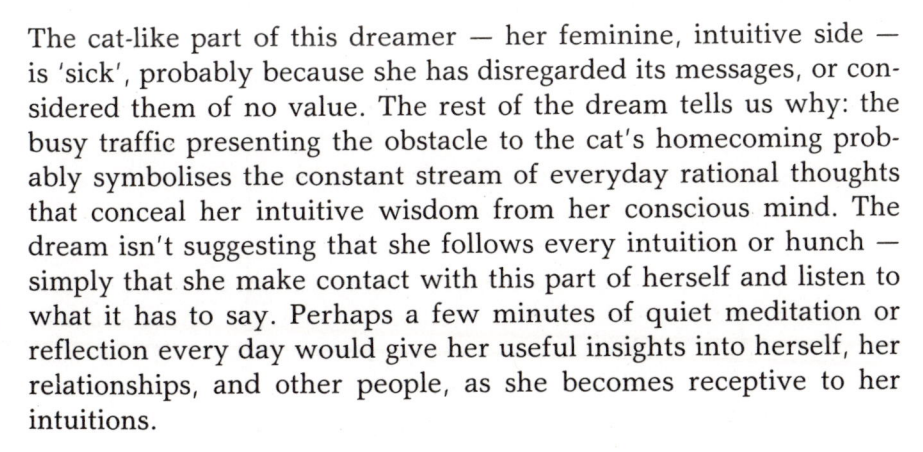

The cat-like part of this dreamer — her feminine, intuitive side — is 'sick', probably because she has disregarded its messages, or considered them of no value. The rest of the dream tells us why: the busy traffic presenting the obstacle to the cat's homecoming probably symbolises the constant stream of everyday rational thoughts that conceal her intuitive wisdom from her conscious mind. The dream isn't suggesting that she follows every intuition or hunch — simply that she make contact with this part of herself and listen to what it has to say. Perhaps a few minutes of quiet meditation or reflection every day would give her useful insights into herself, her relationships, and other people, as she becomes receptive to her intuitions.

Dogs

Sometimes dream animals can symbolise a particular quality that we associate with the animal in real life, such as great persistence or loyalty appearing in the dream in the form of the family dog.

> My terrier had a bone that he wouldn't let anyone near. It was old and mouldy but he was hanging on to it grimly, and wouldn't give it up.

The dog here represents the dreamer's 'doggedness'. Something — perhaps a job or friendship — is becoming old and mouldy, but she is refusing to let go, even though this would seem to be the best course of action.

The animal's behaviour is a good clue to its meaning. Sometimes dogs, common dream symbols, can be aggressive and threatening. In this case, they usually point to feelings of aggression in the dreamer, directed towards the object of the hostility in the dream.

Fish

Fish live in water, and symbolise the contents of the subconscious mind.

Fish live in water, and therefore symbolise the contents of the subconscious mind (see **Water**, page 111). Going fishing can be a theme in the dreams of people who are interested in their inner workings.

> I was fishing off a jetty when I hooked the most enormous fish — it was a monster! I struggled with it for a while, but eventually it broke the line and got away.

All of us have characteristics we'd rather not admit to — vengefulness, manipulativeness, greed, dependency, pig-headness or violent temper, for example. Because we prefer not to acknowledge these tendencies in ourselves, they sink into the subconscious. Unfortunately, once there, they don't go away, but can actually gather strength and come out at times of stress and in our dreams. One of the tasks of growing in self-understanding is to come to terms with, and modify, these negative qualities.

Apparently this dreamer is battling with one of the 'monsters' of her subconscious mind. She does her best but can't land it — that is, bring it to the dry land of conscious awareness, where she will be able to fully understand her motives and feelings. If she continues to pursue, or try to understand this 'monster', then she will probably dream of catching it at some point. Often the fish that's landed after great struggle is quite small and inconsequential: the characteristic we so condemned ourselves for turns out to be a damp squib when understood and dealt with consciously.

Horses

Horses in dreams represent either sexual passion or life energy in general.

> I dreamed I had two horses. One was called Michael, the other was called Rick. My horse, Michael, was very frisky, and lots of fun to ride. I would go for very long, enjoyable rides on him. The other one, Rick, I would ride because I knew he needed the exercise, but he was rather headstrong and prone to bolt. The funny thing is — Rick is my husband's name, Michael is the name of my ex-boyfriend.

This dream makes a very entertaining comparison between the sexual performance of the dreamer's husband and ex-boyfriend. If the dreamer recognises that there are aspects of lovemaking with her husband that she doesn't enjoy as much as she could, perhaps she can tactfully explore with him some ways of improving their sex life.

> I was on an adventure holiday where we rode horses — the tour was with 'The Galloping Mountaineers'! We got on our horses in the morning and galloped up hills all day — my horse was tireless. The view from the top was glorious.

The dreamer's energy and passion for life are represented here by the tireless horse. Her enthusiasm carries her to the heights and the rewards — the views from the top — are magnificent.

On the other hand, dreaming of a tired old nag that can barely lift one hoof after the other, suggests depleted passions and lack of zest for life, indicating the need for a holiday, change of diet, or a new interest to renew the vital energies.

Dreaming of a tired old nag suggests depleted passions and lack of zest for life.

Snakes

Snakes in dreams usually refer to either sexuality (the classic phallic symbol) or to intuitive wisdom.

> I was sitting on the couch in the lounge room with my boyfriend when suddenly snakes started crawling out from underneath the cushions. They were everywhere, slithering out and all over the floor. I was terrified; I jumped up and screamed, and my boyfriend tried to kill them, but there were too many.

Since the dreamer is sitting with her boyfriend, this dream of snakes would refer to her deep feelings about sex. Clearly she is afraid of her sexual feelings, and since her boyfriend gets busy trying to kill the snakes — that is, sexuality — he's probably scared too. Perhaps she fears that she will be overwhelmed by her sexuality, or has been brought up to believe that sexual feelings in women are wrong, or is afraid of the vulnerability that can come with lovemaking. It's important that she becomes consciously aware of her fear (the fact that she has had this strong dream indicates that she has been suppressing the fear) and if she trusts her boyfriend enough, then tells him about it so that he approaches sex at a pace and in a way that does not overwhelm her.

Snakes can also refer to wisdom.

> I was out in the bush when I almost stepped on a snake that I hadn't seen. I was scared at first, but the snake just looked at me quite calmly, then slithered away. The amazing thing was that it had really bright blue eyes.

Perhaps this dreamer is scared of her own native wisdom. She may have been told when she was growing up that she was not clever, so is not aware of her intelligence even when it's right under her nose. The dream is now drawing it to her attention. The colour blue, in dreams, also usually refers to intelligence and reasoning ability, so the snake's eyes are repeating the message from the subconscious mind: that the dreamer should be aware of her own intellect.

Spiders

Spiders usually refer to the dreamer's mother.

Spiders usually refer to the dreamer's mother. Even if our mothers are or were everything we might consciously wish for, and the relationship we have, or had, is excellent, dreaming of spiders is often the subconscious mind's perception of a darker side to our mother's nature. Perhaps this takes the form of an unwillingness on her part to let go and allow us our independence; a subtle interfering in our affairs; or an undermining of values or attitudes that are different from her own.

Wild Animals

The big cats symbolise the passionate, untamed side of the dreamer's nature.

The big cats — lions, tigers, panthers and so on — symbolise the wild, fierce, passionate, untamed side of the dreamer's nature. In our society, however, these qualities have small opportunity for expression. We tend to value reliability, stability and respectability instead, and our inner lions and tigers lie dormant.

> I was in my living room. There were lions and tigers with me, lying on the floor in front of the gas heater while I did my knitting. It was very cosy.

Sometimes our inner passions can be stirred up — often in reaction to too domesticated, tame an existence; an attempt by someone else to dominate us; or a sexual attraction to someone who is not our regular partner. This can be very inconvenient, and we may try to shut these passions out, resulting in a dream like the following.

> I was in the jungle. A huge, man-eating tiger was trying to break down the door of my bamboo hut. I was terrified, and tried to barricade the door, but I felt it was only a matter of time before it got me.

This dream is not indicating that we should let our passions rule our lives. This would be equivalent to opening the door to the tiger and being eaten up. But the tiger — our anger, drive for autonomy, or our sexual desire — needs to be consciously acknowledged and understood. In this dream, it is trying to break down the door to draw the dreamer's attention to it, so that she can understand her needs and take some appropriate action to meet them. This action might involve, for example, freeing herself of unnecessary restraints, taking a stand on an important matter or enlivening a stale sexual relationship. Having achieved its desired results, the dream tiger can then return to the jungle where it belongs and no longer disturb the dreamer with such a terrifying nightmare.

Other Animals
The meaning of other kinds of dream animals can be understood if we look at everyday language about them: RATS may refer to cunning, underhand or dirty aspects of ourselves or others; PIGS can be gluttonous or male chauvinist; ELEPHANTS never forget and so may refer to long-past experiences that have relevance to the present. (See also **Birds**, page 46 and **Insects**, page 74.)

ANTIQUES
Antiques represent our attitudes from the past, or traditional ways of thinking.

> I was in a house filled with antique furniture. I think it had belonged to my mother. Some of it was in excellent condition — other pieces needed work, and some needed throwing out altogether.

Antiques represent our attitudes from the past, or traditional ways of thinking.

The antique furniture of the dream refers to the dreamer's inherited attitudes — the dream even tells us that they came to the dreamer from his mother. Some of them have value for him today, others need change and still others are worn out and have no part to play in modern life. The dreamer can probably, with a little thought, work out which area of his life — perhaps sex, relationships, self-discipline or work — the attitudes are about.

BABIES — See People

BICYCLES

Dreaming of bicycle riding indicates a slow, relaxed stage in the dreamer's life journey.

Bicycle riding represents a relatively slow and relaxed stage in the dreamer's journey through life, as does walking. Here the context gives a further clue to the meaning of the dream: if the dreamer is cycling or walking down a peaceful country lane, then this mode of life seems suited to her circumstances. If, on the other hand, she's battling through peak-hour traffic with trucks and buses, then perhaps her preferred pace of living is at odds with the pressures and demands of her present situation.

Riding a bike, like other kinds of riding (for example, on a horse) can also have sexual associations. The manner and direction of the cycling would give an idea of how we are managing our sexuality and our energy in general.

BIRDS

Birds represent the imagination and 'flights of fancy'.

Birds represent the imagination, 'flights of fancy' and the wish or ability to soar above one's problems. Sometimes they can refer to the dreamer as a 'free spirit'.

> I dreamed I saw a bird trapped in a room. It was flying all around, trying to get out. I opened the windows, but it still couldn't escape.

The trapped bird probably symbolises the dreamer, who may find her freedom and desire to soar limited by a dreary routine or other circumstances. Even when offered an escape route, she stays trapped. Perhaps despite her longing for freedom, she is afraid of leaving the safety of her familiar world.

On the other hand:

> I dreamed I saw a flock of wild birds heading north for winter. They were so high and so beautiful, just doing what was right for them instinctively.

Presumably this dreamer is also learning to follow her instincts about what is right for her, and to do her equivalent of heading north for winter — perhaps finding a warm emotional climate for herself.

Different birds can have particular meanings.
A CHICKEN might refer to the dreamer's lack of courage in a matter.
A GOOSE may be a silly person or decision, or if wild, may represent the soul.
A PEACOCK may represent a beautiful strutting man.
An EAGLE is the sharp-eyed, perceptive side of the dreamer.
A CANARY is tame, harmonious and decorative. Sometimes it refers to telling tales about other people.
An OWL can refer to wisdom, and sometimes to the departed soul of a dead person.
A BLACK BIRD, if rather sinister, can represent the dark, shadowy side of the dreamer. Sometimes a crow can represent a priest or nun.

BLACK — See Colours

BLOOD

Blood represents our life energy. Dreaming of a blood test might indicate that we are assessing our own physical and emotional strength. Bleeding suggests that we are feeling drained by a situation — the context will give us further information. A blood transfusion is a gift of energy and support to the recipient.

BOATS

Water represents the subconscious mind in dreams and so boats show us how we are dealing with our deepest motives, impulses and emotions, from the point of view of our small floating island of consciousness.

Is the boat seaworthy? If it is leaky, then perhaps the subconscious mind is filtering through in the form of unexplained moods or compulsive actions. Is it a tiny boat being tossed about in a huge sea? Perhaps we feel in danger of being overwhelmed by our feelings, or at the mercy of forces outside our control. Is it a luxury liner? Then we feel safe and comfortable in our voyage through life.

Are we floating peacefully on a tranquil lake? Shooting the rapids? Speeding down a river in a power-boat? All these images are metaphors for our relationship with ourselves.

Water represents the subconscious mind in dreams. Boats show us how we are dealing with our deepest impulses and emotions.

THE BODY

Body language is often used as a means of communication in dreams.

The body has a language of its own which is often used as a means of communication in dreams. Generally the body represents the whole person, including the mind, instincts and personality, while individual parts of the body have their own meaning.

The abdomen, or belly, is, naturally enough, the home of the 'gut' feelings. Our language reflects this concept, as we 'swallow our anger', get an 'upset stomach' when we are distressed, or feel 'churned up with emotion'.

Swallowing something quite bizarre in a dream, such as a snake or other animal or object, can refer to swallowing, or trying to repress, the emotion represented by whatever's been taken in (e.g. sexuality, fear, anger or grief).

Arms and Hands

Arms and hands represent our ability to reach out to others, in love or in anger.

> I dreamed that my arms were paralysed. I felt really frightened and unable to handle anything. I knew I had to contact my husband for help, but I couldn't dial his number to phone him at work.

This dreamer feels she 'can't handle' reaching out to others for help and support. Perhaps she feels too vulnerable, or afraid that her approaches will be rejected. But out of this fear she has become powerless. She feels too emotionally paralysed to communicate her need even to her husband — in the dream she cannot get through to him.

The paralysis of the dreamer's arms represents her being stuck between her need for love and her fear of rejection. In this situation, communication is her only way out — she knows she must contact her husband for help, and so must muster all her courage to tell him how she feels and what she needs: she must reach out.

Eyes

Eyes refer to our 'inner vision' — our ability to perceive the underlying meaning of events and experiences. Having watery eyes suggests that our wisdom is clouded by emotion; whilst having a speck or some other irritation in the eyes indicates that we are unable or unwilling to see things as they really are.

Eyes in dreams refer to our 'inner' vision.

Hair

Hair, since it comes out of the head, often refers to the other product of that part of the body, our thoughts.

Having a haircut can represent disciplining and arranging one's ideas, while a wild hairstyle would symbolise wild ideas.

Hair also refers to power. A dream haircut which leaves us dismayed and upset probably indicates a sense of lost power and is inviting us to review our lives, to see where we are failing to express and defend ourselves, and take responsibility for our actions (see Teeth, page 51).

Dyeing our hair is another common dream theme, and reveals the wish to express ourselves in a particular way. Red hair indicates a desire to express passion and strong emotion; dark hair shows that we want to express our earthiness and hidden power; blonde hair shows that we want to be seen as 'light', nice, and socially acceptable.

Head

The head is the home of the mind, of our thoughts and ideas. Thinking needs to be balanced by feeling, intuitive perception and action, so a head that is overly prominent, or decorated with an odd hat, can indicate that the dreamer, or the person being dreamt about, places too much weight on rational thoughts at the expense of the other modes of being.

On the other hand, a wound to the head, or even beheading, may suggest that the dreamer has been carried away by feelings or impulsive action.

A wound to the head may suggest that the dreamer has been carried away by feelings or impulsive action.

Legs and Feet

Legs and feet represent our contact with the ground. Dreams about them show how well we are grounded — that is, in touch with reality. Dreams that our legs are numb or injured, for instance, suggest that our contact with life as it really is, is somehow lacking. Perhaps there are difficult aspects of our work or relationships that we are avoiding because we fear that if we look too closely, then some unpalatable action will be required of us. Legs and feet are also our means of standing our ground, and can refer to independence and our ability to take a stance in the world.

> I dreamed I had to wear some really horrible, tight shoes. They were so uncomfortable that I couldn't walk properly and had to crawl round the floor.

Something is preventing this dreamer from standing on her own two feet — from supporting herself emotionally, and perhaps financially, too. The shoes probably represent a constricting and limiting set of ideas she has about herself — that she is incapable of looking after herself for example. The dream is inviting her to look at the limitations she feels she has and see what she can do to stand up for herself.

Nose

The nose in dreams refers to our ability to tune in to our own inner guidance.

Following one's nose means to follow one's intuition, so the nose in dreams refers to our ability to tune in to our own inner guidance. We 'smell a rat' when we intuitively suspect that something untoward is going on; we may smell flowers in a dream when we have a hunch that a relationship or a project is about to blossom.

Right Versus Left Side

The right side of the body traditionally represents the rational, assertive aspect of the personality, whilst the left side refers to the intuitive, feeling aspect. Dreams where one side of the body is bigger or stronger indicate that the functions represented by that side are more developed. Dreams where one side of the body is wounded or ill suggest that the psychological functions it represents need attention.

Skin

Skin is the boundary between the body and the world and so refers to our sensitivity to others. Having unusually thin skin in a dream indicates that we are particularly vulnerable to others and perhaps oversensitive to their opinions and ideas.

Thick skin on the other hand reveals an insensitivity to the world, perhaps an unwillingness to appreciate other people's vulnerability and a consequent crassness in our dealings with them.

Teeth

Teeth often represent power in dreams — our ability to express and defend ourselves.

In dreams teeth often represent our ability to express and defend ourselves.

> I dreamed I was in a restaurant with my husband when to my horror, my teeth started falling out. I had a mouthful of teeth which I was spitting out into a handkerchief.

Dreams like this are extremely common and refer to the tendency many of us have to give our power away to other people.

We do this in a number of ways: we accept blame and feel guilty when this is inappropriate (the above dreamer, for example, had accepted the blame for her husband's taking up smoking again); we assign responsibility for our lives to the government or our spouses or families, becoming victims of circumstance rather than the determining force in our lives ('I can't leave my job because of the retirement benefits I'll get in eleven years'; or 'I can't leave my marriage because the children are too young'); we avoid expressing our feelings of anger, sadness, fear and need; and we avoid defending ourselves when attacked verbally, because we are afraid to confront others, and fear the loss of love and approval that our words might bring.

All these are ways in which we make ourselves powerless in life and relationships — and dreams of falling teeth are the subconscious mind's way of drawing our attention to what we're doing. An assertiveness training course can be a helpful first step towards regaining our 'teeth'.

Weight

GETTING FAT can refer to pregnancy.
GETTING THIN refers to one's emotional state. Perhaps a lack of emotional or sexual nourishment in the dreamer's life has led to a feeling of inner starvation, represented in the dream by losing weight.

BLUE — See Colours

BOMBS

Bombs indicate the need for change in the dreamer. Perhaps someone in the dreamer's life has 'dropped a bombshell' which requires that the dreamer adapt to new circumstances. Or maybe the dreamer is a little sluggish and needs a bomb put under her. Or a nuclear bomb has, figuratively speaking, changed the dreamer's entire inner landscape. The distress experienced in such a dream is the feeling of loss of familiar ways of thinking and being — the comfort of old ways.

BRIDE — See **Marriage**

BRIDGES

Bridges represent the transition between two ways of being.

Bridges represent the transition or connection between two ways of being. The land on the other side of the bridge may hold something that is very precious to the dreamer so that the task in the dream is to cross the bridge and retrieve it. Or:

> I was standing beside a river in flood looking back at a bridge I'd crossed. It was a rickety old wooden thing. Suddenly a wave carrying old logs and debris came down the river and completely swept the bridge away. I felt that this was the right thing to happen.

Some change has occurred in this dreamer's life, and there is no going back. Perhaps he has resigned from his job, or given up a relationship that wasn't working. Whatever it was, it's now in the past, and however difficult it may have been to make the crossing, the dreamer is happy with his decision.

BUILDINGS

A breathtaking castle could represent the worldly or spiritual heights we long to reach.

Buildings represent an aspect of the dreamer. While houses (see **Houses**, page 72) refer to the body or the personality of the dreamer as a whole, other buildings reveal a specific role that we play in life, or one that we might aspire to. A breathtaking castle or cathedral could represent the worldly or spiritual heights we long to reach. An office building might reveal our role in the business world, while school buildings could show us our attitude towards learning.

At other times, the nature of the building is unimportant, and it appears simply as a backdrop to the events of the dream.

BUS

Bus travel is a mundane way of making our way through life and so represents an ordinary, everyday aspect of our way of being. Buses in dreams often form the background for other events, rather than being particularly significant in themselves. For example, the destination may be important (see **Places**, page 98) or our fellow passengers might be the focus of the dream.

CAGES

Cages have a similar significance to prisons in dreams. (See **Prisons**, page 99).

CAMERA

'The camera doesn't lie' goes the saying — and cameras in dreams appear when we need to have a close look at the truth. The photographer in the dream might be the part of us which is impartial, carefully and accurately recording events in our lives. If the photographer is taking pictures of the wrong things or the photos are distorted, then our view of the situation might be distorted as well.

Some primitive tribes have believed that the camera and the process of being photographed steal their souls. If we feel anxious about being photographed in the dream then perhaps we feel some modern-day equivalent — a fear of losing our independence, perhaps, or of having to expose truths that we do not wish to reveal.

Cameras appear in dreams when we need to have a close look at the truth.

Photos

Photographs in an album represent the past, and our memories of the people and events depicted.

CARS

Cars usually represent the body or personality of the dreamer. A problem with the car may indicate some physical problem or general stress in the life of the dreamer.

> I dreamed several times that my car was overheating. I'd be driving along and glance at the temperature gauge and see that the needle was pointing to the red section.

Somehow the dreamer herself is getting 'overheated' in her waking life. Perhaps she is angry about something and hasn't consciously registered what it is, or is sexually frustrated, or is simply overloaded with responsibilities and feeling highly stressed. The dream shows that she needs to examine her life to find the source of the tension and either make the necessary changes or learn to relax.

> I was backing the car out of the garage when the brakes and the steering failed. The car just rolled off, out of control. I was terrified.

Something is out of control in this dreamer's life. It may be her eating or spending habits, or some other kind of compulsive behaviour which sometimes takes over, against her conscious will. Alternatively, it may be a relationship where she has let someone else take control of her life, perhaps a dominating parent or husband.

If there is someone else in the car, the dream refers to the dreamer's relationship with that person.

> I was driving along with my girlfriend. Every time we came to a red light she would try to get out, and I would have to persuade her to stay in the car.

Stopping for a red light probably refers to a temporary halt in the relationship due to some conflict. Apparently this dreamer's girlfriend doesn't like confrontations and tries to leave the relationship whenever they argue.

Motorbikes and Trucks

These have similar meanings to cars. Dreaming of driving a TRUCK would indicate feelings of strength, and the capacity to carry a heavy load.

The condition of the MOTORBIKE reveals its significance. Does it fly up hills effortlessly giving the dreamer a feeling of freedom and power? Or is it sluggish, exposed and uncomfortable, reflecting the dreamer's everyday state?

CATASTROPHES

Catastrophes in dreams refer to enormous changes taking place within.

Catastrophes in dreams refer to enormous changes taking place within the dreamer. Although they are usually frightening, they do not foretell doom and disaster in everyday life — the fear we feel is a natural response to great change, change which may in fact be very positive.

CATS — See **Animals**

CEMETERY

Cemeteries contain whatever is dead and buried, so often refer to the past. Perhaps there is some incident from the past which we thought we had finished with, yet in the cemetery it can return to haunt us.

Cemeteries can also refer to our thoughts of the dead, particularly if we are there to visit a particular grave.

Sometimes cemeteries refer to our fear of death. The emotion of the dream — fear, awe, sadness or curiosity — will provide further information to help us with our interpretation.

CHILDREN — See People

CIRCLES — See Shapes

CIRCUS

A circus or carnival is often a representation of the dreamer's life at the moment — all noise, colour, showmanship and chaos. If, on the other hand, it is confusing or overwhelming, then the dreamer is being invited to make order out of the chaos. If it is mysterious or frightening, then it may be reflecting a part of the dreamer which longs for a gypsy life of freedom and excitement, which the dreamer rejects, perhaps because of fear of the consequences of expressing it.

A circus or carnival often represents the dreamer's life at the moment — all noise, colour, showmanship and chaos.

CITY

A city is a large gathering of buildings and houses, which themselves represent people, and therefore refers to the community of which the dreamer is a part. The dream reveals the dreamer's relationship to the community — perhaps living right at its centre, or on its fringes, longing to return to it, or escape from it.

CLIMBING

Climbing stairs or mountains, or ascending by a lift or escalator or hot air balloon, refers to going up in the world — in a career or business, in the achievement of some personal goal, or even in a spiritual pursuit.

Sometimes it can indicate sexual attraction or excitement, especially if the dreamer sees lovemaking as a 'conquest' of the partner.

CLOTHING

Clothes in dreams represent our roles in life. As with our clothing and physical presentation, we can put ourselves across to others in many different ways. Dreams about clothing give us a clue as to how well our life roles fit our nature.

> I dreamed I had a very elegant, but tight-fitting suit on, and high heels. I was walking through a park, and my skirt was so tight I couldn't walk up the slopes properly. Also my high heels kept sinking into the grass.

This dreamer's clothes reveal the role she has taken on — stylish, feminine, but very restrictive. Her mobility and flexibility are severely limited by the attitudes and beliefs she is holding. Maybe she feels she must be elegant and in control in all situations, and isn't able to relax and enjoy herself. The high heels sinking into the grass show how bogged down she has become by her self-imposed limitations, and the dream generally is inviting her to loosen up.

Unsuitable clothing is another common dream symbol, indicating that the dreamer is taking a role or set of values into an inappropriate context.

> In my dream I caught the bus to go to work wearing only my dressing gown. I felt really embarrassed!

Dressing gowns are worn at home, and so this dreamer is presumably taking her domestic role to the office. Perhaps she fusses over her colleagues or tidies up after other people unnecessarily. Some part of her is beginning to see that her actions are unsuited to the work environment, and trying to draw this to her attention in a dream.

Very masculine clothes on a woman, or feminine clothes on a man, or old-fashioned items, reveal the subconscious mind's perception of an individual's role. One dreamer saw his wife in a whalebone corset, indicating that he thought her rigid, inflexible and out-of-date.

One dreamer saw his wife in a whalebone corset, indicating that he thought her rigid, inflexible and out-of-date.

COLOURS

Different dream researchers hold conflicting views about whether we dream in colour. Some hold that only one-third of our dreams are in colour — others that all dreams are in colour, but like the dreams themselves, not all the colours are recalled.

It's only when colours are particularly vivid, however, that we pay close attention to them and that they are likely to be important in interpreting the dream.

Colours traditionally hold particular meanings, but if the interpretation given here doesn't seem to fit, the dreamer's own intuition can serve as a guide to their significance.

Black

Black refers to the dark, hidden aspects of our lives and characters.

> I dreamed there was a knock at my door. I looked through the peephole and saw a woman in a black dress and was too scared to let her in.

Black refers to the dark, hidden aspects of our lives.

This visitor probably represents some quality in the dreamer which has been unconscious, but is now requesting admission to her conscious awareness.

Perhaps it is the expression of power in the form of leadership ability, perhaps it is passion or earthiness. The dreamer has reached a time in her life when she is ready to deal with this aspect of herself but is as yet afraid to face it, probably fearing disapproval or confrontation from others if she allows it into her life.

Black also refers to gloom and depression. If the dark sides of our characters are not brought into consciousness and the 'light', and allowed expression in a socially acceptable way, then depression can be the result. We feel ourselves to be stale, stuck, frustrated and unhappy out of our subconscious desire to feel and express our emotions and find fulfillment of our needs.

So if we do not act on a dream like the one above, by understanding what it represents and taking steps to bring our hidden qualities to light, then the colour black can also presage a period of depression.

Blue

Blue represents the intellect and everything that is associated with it, such as thoughts, ideas, rationality and logic.

Blue represents the intellect.

> I dreamed I went into the office of my new boss. He had sprayed the floor with some bright blue slippery stuff, so it was very hard to keep my footing.

According to this dreamer's subconscious perceptions, his boss has some slippery ideas — perhaps reasoning and justifications which are sound on first hearing but which lack 'firm grounding' in reality.

Objects of various kinds are given further meaning by their colour: blue flowers might mean the blossoming of creative ideas; a dog on a blue leash might refer to the curbing of the animal instincts by the mind's ideas about how they should be expressed.

Green

Green is the colour of vitality and of living things. Vivid green usually represents growth and energy in the dreamer. Occasionally

Green is the colour of vitality and of living things.

it can refer to innocence and naivete, as it does in everyday language, and now and again to jealousy (the so-called 'green-eyed monster').

Pink
Pink refers to the more tender emotions, and also to romance and falling in love.

Purple
Purple refers to spiritual matters.

Red

Anger and strong sexual feelings are often symbolised by red objects.

Red represents the passions. Anger and strong sexual feelings can be symbolised by red objects, with the context revealing the precise meaning; making a bed with red sheets, for instance, plainly indicates sexual excitement or intentions.

> I dreamed I was having a tug-of-war with my neighbour's bulldog, each of us pulling on an end of a piece of red cloth.

On waking, this dreamer's first thought was of the expression 'a red rag to a bull' and he applied it to the interpretation of this dream. This phrase means to be provocative and stir up confrontation — the bulldog of the dream was a substitute for the bull of the expression, but the dream indicated to him that in his provocative behaviour in everyday life, he was a 'fight looking for somewhere to happen'.

The colour red, representing blood, also frequently appears in the dreams of menstruating women.

White

White is a symbol of innocence. Dreams of dirtied white often have sexual associations.

White is a symbol of innocence. Dreaming of a white house indicates the dreamer's sense of her own integrity and purity.

Dreams of dirtied white often have sexual associations.

> I dreamed I was on my way to my wedding when a dog jumped up on me and left muddy prints all over my white dress. I felt very distressed.

This dreamer probably comes from a family where a very high value is placed on the virginity of the bride, yet her sexual instincts (represented by the dog) seem to have got the better of her good intentions, and now she feels soiled. Her distress comes out of her guilt, her feeling that she has done the wrong thing. The dream, like all those where the dreamer feels guilty, is inviting her to let go of the judgements she has made of her actions and forgive herself.

Yellow and Gold
Yellow and gold refer to illumination, understanding or intuition about a person or situation.

Yellow and gold refer to illumination or intuition about a person or situation.

> I dreamed that I was in a theatre with a young man wearing bright yellow coveralls. While we watched the show, he went up to the front and took photographs of the actors. Later he came back and said to me: 'The camera never lies'.

The young man in yellow represents this dreamer's capacity to intuitively understand what's going on in the theatre of her life. Like the camera which 'never lies', this capacity can enable the dreamer to see clearly and objectively through the roles of the 'players' in her life, the parts they are acting out and why. The dream is encouraging her to listen to and trust her intuition.

COOKING — See Food

CRESCENTS — See Shapes

CROSS — See Shapes

CROSSROADS
Crossroads or a fork in the road reveal that the dreamer has a choice of life paths. It's common to know what lies ahead in each road when the choice is being made — that is, when the dreamer is standing at the intersection.

> I was standing at a fork in the road. One path led down to where I live, the other up to a place with the most beautiful gardens and trees, and houses that were out of this world.

One road leads to the everyday world of work and family life, where this dreamer lives, and the other to a place of beautiful, but unreal, visions. As the dreamer says, it was 'out of this world', that is, not part of normal reality. He seems to have two ways of being: his life in the real world, and his life in his beautiful fantasy world. Since he has access to such a rich inner landscape, it would be fruitful to bring it into his everyday life, which by contrast must be rather dull. He could pursue some creative interest, either in work, if that's possible, or in some hobby, such as painting his inner visions.

In dreams, the RIGHT HAND PATH, traditionally refers to a life of 'right action', of duty and responsibility, and avoiding temptation.

The LEFT HAND PATH refers to a life where individuals make decisions based on their own sense of what is right for them, rather than conventional wisdom. It's considered riskier, in that there is more opportunity for mistakes and failures. Neither is more correct than the other — it's for the individual to make the choice.

DEATH

Dreams of death fall mainly into three categories: a prediction or expectation of our own death; 'experiencing' our own death; and predicting another person's death or having it occur.

Dreams of death, our own or someone else's, almost never literally foretell the future. Instead they are usually about a symbolic death — a change of some kind — and can actually be quite positive.

Dreaming of our own approaching death refers to a major change in who we are — our attitudes, roles and perhaps lifestyle.

> When my marriage was breaking up, I dreamed I went to the doctor with chest pains. He usually calls me by my given name, but in the dream he said, 'Mrs X, you are going to die'. I was surprisingly calm about it until I woke up and thought about it, and became frightened.

The doctor's calling the dreamer by her married name is an important feature of this dream. It indicates that it is her life as a married woman that is coming to an end. At some level, the dreamer already accepts that this is so and that is why she is calm about it in the dream. It is her everyday, waking self that is unaware of the symbolism of the prediction, takes it literally and is frightened by it.

The chest pains of the dream echo the prediction of the death of the marriage. The chest, of course, is the location of the heart, traditionally the place where we feel love. The chest pains refer to the dreamer's pain at the dying of love.

Dreaming of another person's death is also not to be taken literally. Usually it refers to the death of the characteristics or influence represented by that person, that have existed in the dreamer himself. A graphic example is the dream death of a parent.

> I dreamed that my father rang one morning to say that my mother had had a stroke and died in the night. He was distraught, but I felt that I could handle it okay.

From infancy we carry within us our parents' attitudes, instructions and values. It is as if, long after we have left home, there is an inner mother or father looking over our shoulders and telling us how we should be running our lives, criticising us when we act against their values and encouraging us to behave in certain ways.

True maturity requires that we become aware of these inner parents, and release their influence over us, so that we make our life decisions not out of compliance to their wishes, or out of the opposite, rebellion against everything they represent. Instead, we act with genuine independence, behaving in the ways which most enhance our wellbeing, regardless of what our parents would think.

So this dream refers to the death not of the dreamer's real mother, but of his inner mother. Having released her influence, he is on the way towards true maturity and independence. The dream, whilst shocking, is actually very positive.

All dreams of the death of another person can be interpreted in this way. Naturally we fear that such dreams are literally predicting the future, but this is very rarely so. (See also 'Do dreams foretell the future?', page 15.)

Dreaming that we have actually died and can see our own dead body can occur at times of great stress and change. It indicates that it is extremely difficult for us to cope with life at present and that we wish to escape from reality.

Dreams of our own death can occur at times of great stress and change.

Often our self-esteem will be at a low ebb, and we feel there is no-one to turn to for support. Sometimes, it's hard to face up to the depth of our despair and so we do our best to struggle on until a dream like this shocks us into reviewing the situation. Finding someone to talk to — a loving friend or sympathetic counsellor, can help us to find our feet again. (See also **Dead People**, page 92.)

DESCENDING

Descending stairs, or in a lift, can refer to the opposite of climbing — retiring from a career, or winding down activities directed towards achieving personal or even sexual goals (see **Falling**, page 64).

Descending can also refer to an exploration of the subconscious.

> I dreamed I had been at a business meeting. When I left the office, I found that my path led down a very steep hill — it was quite muddy and slippery. When I eventually got to the bottom I saw a school with some young children out in the yard. They were laughing and laughing — I don't know why — and seemed to be really enjoying themselves.

This dream compares the everyday outer world of work and business with an inner journey — a descent to the subconscious. It indicates that it's not an easy path, but shows the dreamer something he might find there — his capacity for childlike playfulness and fun. Perhaps he takes himself and his life too seriously, and the dream is telling him that if he looks within, he will find a surprising ability to enjoy himself.

The descent, in dreams, can take many forms. Sometimes the dream will indicate how it is to be done — through dreamwork or meditation or journal-keeping, for instance. Sometimes, as in the above dream, it will indicate some of what is to be found 'below' — perhaps the turbulent seas of suppressed emotion; an arid desert of despair and hopelessness which the dreamer must bring back to life; or a lost city of amazing treasure.

DESERT

A desert reflects a barren interior landscape, lacking in the emotion represented by water. It can appear in dreams when the emotional life is arid and empty, and indicates the need for the dreamer to reconnect with feelings and reach out for contact with others.

DEVIL

The devil in dreams represents the part of us which we perceive as evil.

The devil in dreams represents the part of the dreamer which he or she perceives as evil. Dreams about the devil are usually very frightening, as we seek to escape from the aspects of ourselves we see as bad, and fear they will overwhelm us.

> I dreamed that Satan came into my kitchen. He was horrible. I chopped him up with my kitchen knife and put him in bags in the freezer but I knew he wasn't dead.

Unpleasant though it is, it's important to face up to those aspects of ourselves that we see as dark and evil. Maybe we think we're not like that until a dream like this shows us that we do have these sides to us.

What might they be, specifically? Perhaps we are angry with someone and fear that our rage is demonic. Or we may have sadistic sexual fantasies which we judge to be wrong. Or wish that someone who hurt us would die.

If it's difficult to identify what the devil in the dream represents to us, then it can help to ask for another dream the following night to explain the symbolism (see Chapter 2). This might take some courage, but the second dream is unlikely to be as frightening as the first — the subconscious mind no longer needs to shock us now that it well and truly has our attention!

In the dream quoted above, it's clear that the dreamer won't be able to get rid of these parts of herself that she judges to be evil by 'putting them on ice'. They may be temporarily out of sight, but are still alive and must be dealt with.

Dealing with them requires, firstly, identifying them: looking at the nature of these inner demons. Secondly, we need to accept that they exist — that we do have these thoughts and feelings, even if we wish we didn't.

Thirdly, we need to understand that thoughts and feelings are not evil in themselves — in fact, often we can't help having them — and that only our *actions* can be judged in this way.

Fourthly, we need to look at what action might be required to resolve the situation that brings up the demonic feelings. Perhaps we can write down how angry we are, or how deeply wounded we feel and allow the part of us that wants revenge to imagine what we might do. Or have a closer look at our sexual fantasies in the cold light of day.

Last of all, laugh about them. Even if they seem awful, shameful and terrifying, find something funny in there. Laughter is a powerful way to self-acceptance, and taking ourselves less seriously is a remarkably effective method for dissolving inner demons.

DOGS — See Animals

EARTHQUAKES

Earthquakes indicate that our old habits and attitudes are falling apart.

Earthquakes indicate that the ground of our old habits and attitudes is falling apart. Perhaps we have deliberately worked on transforming ourselves, or perhaps the events of our lives have forced us to change. Either way, the change seems inevitable and can best be dealt with by being aware of the ways in which we are developing and accepting the new way of being.

EXAMS

Exams represent some kind of test in life, perhaps a job interview, or promotion, perhaps a new sexual relationship where the dreamer feels that a great deal is at stake, or even a medical examination. Dreams about exams often involve forgetting everything we've learned; running very late; realising as we sit down to do the paper that we know nothing about the subject, or even what the subject is, or messing up the test in some other way.

Such dreams simply reflect our anxieties, and never foretell the future. Sometimes when we feel anxious about a matter we try to cheer ourselves up by ignoring our fears. The dream is asking us to consciously take notice of them.

The simplest way to face them squarely is to write them down. Put down on paper your worst fears about your forthcoming 'test' in life. Then go through them one by one to see if they are realistic. Very few of them will be, so reassure yourself on that score. If any of them are realistic, then make whatever preparations are necessary to ensure that these fears are not realised. The dream will not recur.

FALLING

Falling in dreams represents insecurity. The context will provide further clues to interpretation.

Falling in dreams represents the dreamer's insecurity. It may be in a relationship, or in work or in life generally — the context will provide further clues to interpretation.

> I dreamed my boyfriend and I were in a lift which suddenly started to plummet to the ground. I was really scared, and then I started to tell a joke to keep my spirits up. I woke up before we hit the ground.

Since this dreamer is with her boyfriend, the plummeting lift probably represents her insecurity in her relationship. Yet her way of handling it is to tell a joke to keep her spirits up: probably in life she does the same thing by trying to appear cheerful even when she is frightened or upset. Of course this provides temporary relief, but does nothing for the insecurity. The way to deal with this is to develop confidence in her ability to communicate her needs and feelings in the relationship and in her ability to stand alone if necessary.

If the dream of falling seems to relate to insecurity in our career then the solution is a little different. Failing in a career is indeed a major disaster if our self-esteem is based entirely on the ability to succeed at work.

Yet we all need to have a range of areas in which we are competent. Effectiveness in family life, social relationships, money management and creative skills, for example, might be the basis for confidence and self-esteem. Then the prospect of failing in one area is no longer totally shattering — our sense of security is broadly based in ourselves instead of dependent on one aspect of our lives such as work.

In dreams of falling, we often wake before hitting the bottom — our insecurity is often so frightening that we avoid thinking about the consequences of the failed career or relationship.

Yet hitting the bottom can be a positive symbol in a dream, as it refers to facing up to our worst fears.

> I was walking upstairs in an office building with my two children when the railing and some of the stairs collapsed and we fell through the stairwell. I was very frightened, but then we hit the bottom, we were all bruised and shaken but okay. The worst thing was that there was no way out — we were trapped at the bottom of the stairwell. I knew we would have to wait until the next morning before we were found.

This dreamer wants to make her way in the world (going upstairs) but feels insecure about doing this and looking after her children properly too. The 'bottom line', however, the aspect of her conflict which has been hard to face, is the feeling that she is trapped with her children and for some reason may have to wait a while until she is able to get out and about again.

FAMILY

Members of our family usually represent themselves. The dream can provide insights into our attitude towards them, or the relationship in general.

Members of the dreamer's family usually represent themselves, the dream providing insight into the dreamer's attitude towards them, or the relationship in general.

Occasionally they can represent aspects of the dreamer's personality. All of us, for example, have been brought up with some kind of moral code and set of rules for behaviour, and often these values can appear in a dream in the form of a parent.

> In my dream I was reading in my room when my mother (long since dead) came in and told me to put the dinner on for my family. I was surprised and said that we'd just have something light and perhaps they could fix themselves up. Next thing I knew, my mother was in my kitchen putting together a huge production of a meal for us all — typical! I felt rather guilty and put out.

Her mother represents the part of this dreamer which holds to traditional values about feeding and caring for her family. Consciously, the dreamer has a relaxed attitude towards such things, allowing her family to fend for themselves. Yet subconsciously she feels guilty about not following her mother's ways. The dream is inviting her to look at and let go of these guilty feelings and then decide what's best for herself and her family, regardless of what her mother's values might have been.

Brothers, sisters, aunts, uncles and cousins can also refer to aspects of the dreamer. In interpreting the dream, we can look at the role they take in the dream or consider what they represent to us.

Grandparents, when not standing for themselves, represent the values of an older generation, often presented so that we can review them consciously and decide which ones still hold for us in the modern world.

FIRE

Fire usually represents the heat of the emotions, particularly sexual desire. It may be a pleasant hearth fire, symbolising domestic sexual pleasure, or a bonfire, or a raging, out-of-control bushfire which prompts the dreamer to flee — something which the dreamer probably does in real life when confronted with overwhelming passion!

Fighting the fire reveals that the dreamer is attempting to control strong emotions and desires.

Fire can also represent a cleansing or purification.

Fire usually represents the heat of the emotions, particularly sexual desire.

> Looking back, I realise that during my teenage years at home I was always compromising and giving in to my mother's whims because she was sick. Eventually my father decided to get a full-time nurse, and when I was twenty-one I decided to move to another part of the city. I had had it with compromising and decided that I would do what I wanted to do and no longer live just to please others. The night after I moved out I dreamed that my parents' house was on fire. There was no-one inside. I was watching from across the road, and instead of feeling upset, I had a great sense of satisfaction, and a feeling of rightness.

The house represents the dreamer as she used to be when she lived there — necessarily submissive to someone else's wishes. By deciding to move out, she is cleansing herself of a way of life which has become distasteful to her and the dream of fire is a satisfying way of purifying herself of the past so she can begin afresh.

Flame

A flame with the emphasis more on its light than its heat can represent the dreamer's spirit, or inner being. It is also often a symbol for the light of consciousness, or illumination about a matter.

Occasionally, it may refer to an 'old flame'.

FISH — See Animals

FLOODS

Floods, like huge ocean waves symbolise the dreamer's fears of being overwhelmed by impulses or feelings. (See **Oceans**, page 86.)

FLOWERS

Flowers generally refer to the blossoming of some aspect of our lives — a friendship, or a new form of creative expression.

Flowers generally refer to the blossoming of some aspect of the dreamer's life, perhaps a friendship, or a new form of creative expression.

Individual varieties of flowers may hold their own significance for the dreamer: one woman who had moved house a great deal noticed that whenever she planted shasta daisies in her garden, the family would move within six months. Later, dreaming of shasta daisies symbolised an impending change of some kind, not necessarily of residence.

However, certain kinds of flowers traditionally hold particular meanings. Dreaming of ROSES suggests the blossoming or desire for romance. FORGET-ME-NOTS may be asking the dreamer to remember something. WILDFLOWERS indicate that whatever is blossoming will do so in its own season and that the dreamer is not required to cultivate the friendship or project for it to develop.

The COLOUR of the flowers may be significant, too. (See **Colours**, page 56.)

DEAD FLOWERS suggest that the dreamer's hopes in a matter have been disappointed.

FLYING

Flying in dreams is often indicative of a wish to evade everyday earthly reality. Perhaps it is tedious and boring, or difficult and burdensome, and flying is a way to avoid its tensions by soaring instead of plodding. The circumstances and location provide more information about the desire to escape.

Flying can also be an attempt to escape aspects of oneself that are hard to face.

> I dreamed I was being chased by an awful, frightening man. The only way I could escape him was to fly up into the air. I could just do it, but he kept trying to grab my ankle to bring me down to earth again.

The awful man probably represents the dreamer's disowned anger or assertiveness (see **Unknown Man**, page 95). She tries to avoid these instincts by flying — perhaps by 'flights of fantasy' — but the time, like the man, is coming close when she will have to face up to them. She may be afraid to do so as yet, for fear of the consequences, such as disapproval, but it is actually desirable that she looks at this aspect of herself: it will bring her 'down to earth' — in other words, help her come to grips with the practical everyday needs of reality.

In a woman's dream, flying with an unknown male companion can also indicate too heavy an emphasis on ideas and thinking. She may enjoy using her intellect, but needs to balance out this way of being by tuning into and expressing her feelings, and taking action where it's required in her life. Flying with her spouse or partner may have this meaning, too. Alternatively, it can show that they 'soar' together — that their relationship has reached the heights of fulfilment.

FOOD AND COOKING

Food, in dreams, represents emotional and sexual nourishment. If the dreamers are the cooks, then the dream will be about the way in which they nourish themselves and others.

Food in dreams represents emotional and sexual nourishment.

> In my dream I was cooking a meal of roast beef and vegetables (I am a vegetarian), for a dinner party. When I served it, I saw that there wasn't enough to go around so I served it out for everyone else and quickly cooked myself a boiled potato.

Like many women, this dreamer looks after the other people in her life, but is not so good at nourishing herself. She probably does things for her family that are uninteresting, or even distasteful to her (symbolised by the roast beef), such as taking them on outings to places that she doesn't like.

The dream indicates that she is getting the bare minimum of emotional, and probably sexual, nurturing. Self-nurturing requires being clear about what we want: this dream is inviting her to look at what would most nourish her (time to herself? An evening out every week? An hour alone with her husband every evening to talk?) and be willing to arrange or ask for it, rather than settling for the emotional 'boiled potato' of life.

A lavish meal, on the other hand, indicates that the dreamer is receiving a great deal of love and attention. Is it too rich? Then perhaps the attention is somehow suffocating. Does she eat at a restaurant and avoid paying? Perhaps she is soaking up the love but is not giving anything back, and feels guilty about that.

Cooking can represent transformation. Perhaps the 'raw' truth about something is unpalatable and indigestible and the dreamer is modifying it into a more acceptable form for someone else.

Cooking can also refer to any kind of project that the dreamer has underway.

> I had a series of dreams about cooking whilst working on a major report for work. In one of the early dreams, I was frustrated and upset because I didn't have all the ingredients. When it was almost finished, I dreamed I cooked and served a very elaborate meal which everyone loved.

The ingredients probably refer to the 'raw materials' for the project, and the elaborate, well-received meal to the finished project.

FORESTS

The meaning of a forest in a dream depends on the dreamer's response to it. If the dreamer feels lost and confused there, then perhaps she 'can't see the forest for the trees' at the moment. On the other hand, if it feels safe and protected, perhaps it reflects either a haven in a time of stress, or a sense of security pervading the dreamer's life.

FRIENDS — See People

FRONT/BACK — See Opposites

FRUIT

When an enterprise is coming to fruition, dreams of orchards, fruit and ripeness may occur. Usually such dreams are very enjoyable. Dreaming of a worm in the apple or some similar flaw probably indicates that there is some unforeseen difficulty with the matter in hand which needs to be identified and dealt with. Often the difficulty can be in the dreamer's own attitudes — perhaps self-doubt or fear of failure.

GARDENS

Gardens represent the inner life of the dreamer and the aspects of the personality that are being 'cultivated'. One dreamer who had just begun to take an interest in her own actions, motives and personal 'growth' dreamed:

> I was looking out into my garden and noticed that it consisted of a straggly, overgrown lawn and a tree. I thought to myself, I really should get to work on this garden — flowers here, vegetables there, shrubs over here and it could be very good.

In other words, she was preparing to cultivate her inner garden.

Dream gardens are often lush and full of flowers and a pleasure to visit. Clues to the details of their meaning can be found in the events that occur there — perhaps a meeting with a person or animal, perhaps a visit to a house or building.

Dream gardens are often lush, full of flowers, and a pleasure to visit.

GREEN — See Colours

GROOM — See Marriage

HATRED

A strong feeling of hatred can come up in a dream when the subconscious mind wants to call our attention to powerful suppressed emotion. In our society, hatred is frowned upon and we are encouraged to forgive. Yet sometimes it's hard to forgive and instead we simply repress our rage against someone we feel has hurt us.

Repressed hatred — even from the distant past — can affect our present relationships and our physical and emotional health in all kinds of ways. A dream where we feel strongly is an indication that a necessary healing process is underway, whereby we consciously acknowledge our feelings and allow them to be released when they have been fully experienced.

This is not to say that we let fly with our anger towards its target. Acknowledging the feeling to ourselves and perhaps writing down everything we can about it, is often sufficient. Further, the target of the hatred in the dream may not be the actual person we are really angry with, but represent someone else. Sometimes the object of hatred may even be a part of ourselves that we are enraged with. Fully understanding and experiencing the hatred is a necessary step to release and forgiveness.

In a dream we can acknowledge our feelings and allow them to be released.

HEATWAVE — See Weather

HOMOSEXUALITY — See Sex

HORSES — See Animals

HOUSES

A house in dreams usually refers to the body or personality of the dreamer, so looking at the nature of the house and its role in the dream gives us useful feedback about ourselves.

It has been estimated that around 40 per cent of our dreams are about houses, or have houses as a major theme.

It has been estimated that around 40 per cent of our dreams have houses as a major theme.

> I dreamed I was in a decrepit old house on a main road with lots of heavy traffic. It had cobwebs in the corners and some of the doors were coming off their hinges. There was dust everywhere and it needed a good clean-out. I was surprised to dream this, as my life was very happy and full at the time.

Since the dreamer's life is working well and she is happy, this dream is likely to refer to her physical condition — run down and in need of a good clean-out! She is being reminded by her subconscious mind to take good care of herself, perhaps through proper diet, exercise and relaxation, as it seems that she has been neglecting to look after herself physically. The busy main road reflects her full life, but that heavy traffic, with its dust and vibration, is like her busy schedule, in that it no doubt puts extra stress on the 'dwelling' of her body.

The size of a house in a dream and the number of rooms in it, gives us a reflection of the development of the personality.

> I dreamed I went back to live in a house I moved out of about three years ago. I was amazed and delighted when I went in to find that some of the rooms were much bigger than they used to be, and there was even an extra room! It was all much lighter and brighter than it used to be, too.

This dream reveals the dreamer's personal development over the last three years. Rooms represent aspects of ourselves, so she has apparently expanded her confidence in some way, perhaps by learning some new skill, or becoming more assertive. She has also discovered some completely new resource within herself (the extra room) over this period — perhaps an ability to deal with people or make money or lead others. Overall, like this dream house, she is generally lighter and brighter than she used to be.

Sometimes rooms in houses, unlike the ones in this dream, are cramped, dark and frightening. These represent aspects of ourselves which we have not sought to develop, often because we judge them to be unacceptable or undesirable. For example, a woman may feel that if she stands up for her rights, then she will be seen as aggressive and pushy. She may then dream of frightening, unknown, locked rooms in her house, and may continue to do so until she accepts that she has the right to take a stand and develop her potential.

PEOPLE in the house usually also refer to aspects of the dreamer, while the FRONT OF THE HOUSE is the personality and appearance that the dreamer presents to the world.

UPSTAIRS ROOMS, especially attics, represent the dreamer's conscious thoughts and ideas, whilst DOWNSTAIRS ROOMS, particularly cellars, refer to the subconscious mind, and often the instincts and emotions. The FRONT AND BACK ROOMS of the house can have the same meanings as upstairs and downstairs respectively.

Occasionally the house symbolises domestic life and family relationships. Dreaming of HOUSE RENOVATIONS and REPAIRS can indicate the need to repair relationships rather than the building itself.

DOORS can represent a means of self-protection. To dream of inadequate locks and intrusion may reveal that we need to learn to stand up for ourselves. Sometimes doors represent a means of escape.

WALLS CLOSING IN may be a symbol of the dreamer's birth. Some psychologists believe that the experiences of the womb and birth register on our subconscious minds at a deep level and stay in our memories throughout life. Some kinds of hypnosis and psychotherapy can bring to light memories of events of pregnancy and birth which the person's mother is able to confirm as having actually occurred. These experiences are thought to have a profound impact on our emotional development. Any impending change or period of transition may remind us subconsciously of birth. It may then trigger a dream of contracting walls, reddish light, a feeling of pressure and suffocation, and perhaps the pulsing noise of the mother's heartbeat.

The eyes are said to be the WINDOWS of the soul, and in dreams windows usually symbolise our way of looking at the world. Closed, they may indicate a closed mind — open, a viewpoint that is open to change. The view from the window can tell us about the dreamer's outlook on life — whether gloomy and depressing or sunny and appealing.

A TEMPLE may refer to the 'temple of the soul' — sometimes the body, sometimes the dreamer's spirit.

ILLNESS

Dreaming of illness can sometimes be an indication that some part of the body needs attention, so a check-up may be the appropriate response.

Dreaming of inadequate locks and intrusion may reveal a need to learn to stand up for ourselves.

Doors can represent a means of self-protection.

Often, however, the illness has a symbolic meaning. A heart attack, for instance, may mean that the dreamer is having problems in loving, perhaps having sacrificed relationships in order to become powerful or rich, or may have been hurt and has closed the heart off to other people. The dream is showing how important it is to lovingly relate to others.

A dream of cancer suggests that something is gnawing away at the dreamer emotionally. Often this is a need to honestly speak one's mind, or to reach out to others for love and support. A stroke or problems with the head indicate that we are mentally overloaded. We need to relax and experience other aspects of ourselves apart from thoughts: expressing or enjoying feelings and physical pleasures such as eating, exercising or making love, or having a holiday, may help turn off our thinking and give us a mental rest.

Often the part of the body affected by illness tells us more about the nature of the problem (see **The Body**, page 48).

INCEST — See **Sex**

INSECTS

Generally, insects represent all those things that 'bug' us, ranging from the cousins staying with us for a week, to the latest tax laws.

Usually the behaviour of the insects reveals who or what they symbolise: do they buzz around and refuse to leave us alone? Do they get into everything in the kitchen? Do they prevent us from getting on with our work? And who or what does this behaviour remind us of?

Butterflies are an exception to this. From ancient times the butterfly has been regarded as a symbol of the human soul.

From ancient times the butterfly has been a symbol of the human soul.

> I dreamed I was given a brooch, in the shape of a butterfly, that was broken in two halves. It was my job to mend it so it was whole again.

Most of us are in some way divided, like this brooch, by our fears, inner conflicts and divergent desires. This dreamer is being invited by her subconscious mind to heal some of her inner splits and make herself whole again.

Other common butterfly dreams include the trapped butterfly, a symbol of the dreamer's inner being that longs for freedom; and the beautiful butterfly in a garden of flowers, symbolising the beauty of a blossoming inner life.

IRONING

Ironing clothes is a symbol for ironing out difficulties. It can appear in dreams when the dreamer's role is 'smoothing' out problems.

JEWELS AND JEWELLERY

Jewels and jewellery represent whatever we value. Dreaming of being given or finding jewellery indicates that the dreamer has received or discovered within, something very precious, such as love, or strength or confidence.

Dreams about losing jewellery are also quite common.

In dreams, jewels and jewellery represent whatever we value.

> Ever since my eldest child was born, I've dreamed occasionally that I've lost my diamond and sapphire engagement ring. I keep it on a bedside table, and sometimes I wake up in the night in a panic, afraid that it's gone.

An engagement ring is a symbol of the love between husband and wife. Perhaps this dreamer fears that since her children were born, something has been lost from her relationship with her husband. The dream is suggesting that she has a good look at her marriage and does whatever is required to bring it to life again.

JOURNEYS AND TRAVELLING

Journeys in dreams reveal how we are travelling through life: the means of transport, the terrain, the circumstances and destination providing detailed feedback on our progress.

KEY

A key represents the solution to a problem, and a means of opening some symbolic door.

A key represents the solution to a problem, and the means to open some symbolic door.

> In my dream, I shared my office with a doctor. When I got to work, I found I didn't have my keys with me, and couldn't get in. It was very frustrating. I had to wait for the doctor to come and open up.

The dream doctor holds the key to 'getting to work' for the dreamer, suggesting that some healing is required before she can accomplish her tasks. The tasks may literally be her work at the office, or some other tasks to do with her relationships or self-development. The healing that is the key to success for her might be physical or emotional.

The dream is showing her that she needs to take the necessary steps to improve her state of wellbeing in order to unlock the door to further progress in her life.

KILLING

Killing a person or animal in a dream, or watching a killing taking place, indicate that we are trying to stifle or kill off some aspect of ourselves.

> I dreamed there was a bikie outside my house, all dressed in black leather and very dangerous. I knew he had a bike chain and a knife. I told him to go away but he refused to leave so I went into the house for my gun and came out and shot him. I had to shoot him several times because he was so strong.

What might the bikie represent to this dreamer? We know that he is strong and dangerous — perhaps he fits the stereotype and is also unprincipled, wild and violent. This, then, is an aspect of the dreamer which she rejects in herself and wants to be rid of. It is an irony of dreams like this that in killing off the violent aspect of ourselves in dreams, we too become violent killers!

I believe that no part of the personality should ever be stifled or killed off, no matter how unpleasant or distasteful it seems at first sight. Every aspect of us has worth, and if squarely faced, can often be transformed into a valuable ally. This bikie, for instance, if confronted and accepted, may become a symbol for that part of us which is able to powerfully defend us, physically or verbally, when we are seriously threatened. His wildness and unpredictability may promote our independence and spontaneity.

So rather than shuddering with distaste at a dream like this we need to explore its potential — to look at the value that the rejected parts of us may have and the ways in which we can assimilate their positive aspects into our lives.

KNIFE

A knife is often a symbol for emotional and sexual penetration, and in a dream reveals the dreamer's attitude towards being emotionally and sexually open.

If the dreamer is frightened and running, then he or she would seem to fear sexuality and intimacy (see also 'Why do I have nightmares?', page 16). If some sort of initiation rite is taking place involving a knife, then perhaps the dream is referring to an initial sexual experience.

A knife might also give us information about our spouse or lover.

A knife is often a symbol for emotional and sexual penetration.

> I was watching my husband cutting up some meat for a barbecue. He was quite methodical and tidy about it — slice, slice and on to the plate. I didn't feel much emotion, but the dream struck me as important and stayed with me.

With the initial clue of the knife, this dreamer felt that the dream referred to her sexual relationship with her husband. As a lover, she found him methodical and reliable, yet somehow she felt that they did not meet emotionally — that he treated her as flesh, or meat, in the language of the dream — without much intimacy or closeness.

After the dream she gave some thought to what she needed in their relationship and broached the subject with him tactfully. She told him how much she enjoyed lying with him quietly before making love and talking 'pillow talk' and how much she liked to look at his face and be looked at during lovemaking. Although he found this difficult, he was willing to try and these simple steps introduced a new closeness to their sexual relationship.

Knives in dreams can also represent cutting away the old. Pruning or slicing may be the subconscious mind's symbols for cleaning up whatever is no longer required in the dreamer's life.

KNOCK

Opportunity knocks in dreams as well as in life and a knock on the door usually comes from a part of us which wants to be let in to have a fuller role in our lives. Letting it in almost always enhances our wellbeing and enjoyment of life.

> My mother and I were having tea in my kitchen when a knock came at the door. I opened it to find two gypsies there. I wanted to let them in, but my mother said not to, so I sent them away.

What do the gypsies represent? To some they might indicate slyness and treachery, indicating that the dreamer needed to acknowledge her own capacity for sneakiness and notice the ways in which she was being sly in work and relationships. But to this dreamer they represented spontaneity, freedom and music. Her mother apparently disapproved of such things and didn't want them in her daughter's life. Yet there's a lot to be said for fun, and this dreamer could benefit from taking up dancing, for instance, or learning to sing — the opportunities that knocked at her door.

LAKES

Lakes usually represent a sanctuary of peace, quiet and tranquillity. Often they can be the goal of a dream journey, or can come to us in a dream at a time of chaos in our waking lives to reassure us that serenity and inner peace can still exist.

LAUGHTER

Laughter is a joyful celebration of life and a great cleanser. In a dream it often comes as a healer of sadness and disappointment leaving us refreshed and cheerful when we awaken.

LAUNDRY

Depending on what we are actually doing with it, laundry can symbolise anything from 'airing our dirty linen' to cleaning up the past to wringing the last drops out of an experience.

> At a time when I had been having some rather noisy arguments with my wife, I dreamed I saw her hanging out clothes and sheets which hadn't been washed. They were quite stained and dirty and I was afraid and embarrassed about the neighbours seeing them.

The dirty clothes and sheets, of course, represent the 'dirt' that has been flying during the dreamer's arguments with his wife. He must have been concerned that the neighbours could hear, and would judge him for having other than a totally sanitised way of being with his wife, and perhaps even a stained and unsavoury past.

LIGHTNING — See **Weather**

LOST

Dreams about getting lost are usually frightening and frustrating. They refer to being lost in everyday life — having taken the wrong track in some way or being unable to reach one's life goals or destination.

> In my dream I was desperately trying to find my way home before **dark**. Yet at every turn I became more and more confused. The streets **were** full of strange buildings, with hardly any people around. The ones I asked for directions couldn't help. I became very distressed and woke crying.

Home is the most common destination of such dreams. It refers to the 'inner home' — being at home with ourselves.

This requires that we come to know ourselves to some extent and learn to follow the inner voice that tells us what is the right thing for us to do, even if it feels a little risky, or seems to go against conventional wisdom. As the dream points out, other people cannot direct us to our inner home.

This dreamer seems to be taking a number of 'turns' or changes of direction in life, without success. Perhaps in her desperation, she is trying anything to relieve the pain of being lost.

But the solution is not to change for its own sake, but to find an inner map. This requires an evaluation of life as it presently is: how are our relationships, our work, health, leisure activities, lifestyle? Do we have a sense of purpose in our lives? Having thus located ourselves on the inner map, we then identify our destination by answering the question: how would we like these aspects of our lives to be? And then identify how we might achieve these goals.

This can sometimes be a challenging process, as radical changes may be required, but often simply requires a re-organisation of our time and priorities.

Being home before dark is a common theme of dreams about being lost. It represents the dreamer's desire to make something of her life before it's too late — before she gives up hope, or depending on her age, before she dies.

Other aspects of the dream provide further information about its

Being home before dark is a common theme of dreams about being lost.

meaning: perhaps the dreamer has taken the 'wrong track'; is travelling by the most complicated route possible instead of going directly to her destination; or perhaps she's lost in her workplace, suggesting that she's in the wrong job.

LOVER — See People

MARRIAGE

Weddings often symbolise a 'union' with something we don't yet have in everyday life.

Dreams about weddings are quite common. Sometimes they reflect the dreamer's wish to marry a particular person, but more often they have the symbolic meaning of a 'union' with whatever we don't yet have or express in everyday life.

> I have been happily married for four years, but recently keep dreaming that I am going to my wedding. I get to the church all excited and see my husband-to-be, and it's someone I don't even know.

An unknown man, in a woman's dream, refers to the so-called masculine qualities in the dreamer herself, such as assertiveness and rationality. The dream indicates that she is more and more able to express these aspects of herself in everyday life — not at the expense of her womanly qualities, but in a way which reflects strength and maturity (see **Unknown Man**, page 95).

Bride

A bride can refer to the essence of the feminine energy within, all of us having both 'masculine' and 'feminine' aspects to us. What she does in the dream is an indication of the direction in which our feminine energy is moving.

> In my dream I arrived at the church for my wedding. I don't know who the bridegroom was, but as I walked up the steps I suddenly got quite upset and thought 'I like my life the way it is — I don't want to get married!'

This dreamer is still developing and enjoying her feminine side — her awareness and expression of her feelings and intuition. She doesn't feel ready to explore the masculine aspects of herself and doesn't want to integrate them into her life. Doing so is a natural step in every woman's life, but only when she is ready.

A bride, like marriage, can also signify a new beginning of some kind.

Bridegroom
A bridegroom has a parallel meaning to that of a bride — an indication of the direction in which our masculine energy is moving.

White Wedding Dress
The white wedding dress is a symbol of innocence. If, in the dream, it has been handed down to the dreamer by her mother or grandmother, this indicates her acceptance of traditional values.

If it is soiled or stained, this suggests that the dreamer is feeling guilty about something she's done — probably sexual — and should rethink her values. She needs to accept her sexual needs and behaviour as a normal and desirable part of who she is.

MIRRORS
Mirrors reflect our way of appearing to ourselves and others. Sometimes our dream reflection may show us as we normally look; sometimes we may appear more beautiful, indicating that we under-rate our attractiveness; sometimes we may look quite odd, the kind of oddness revealing our subconscious mind's perception of how we are at present (see **The Body**, page 48).

A white wedding dress handed down from the dreamer's mother or grandmother indicates her acceptance of traditional values.

> The night after I'd had a big fight with my wife, I dreamed she came to me with a mirror and held it up so I could see my face. I looked the way I usually do.

During their argument, this dreamer's wife had presumably given him some feedback on how she was seeing him. The dream indicates that she had shown him as an 'accurate reflection' of himself.

MONEY

Money in dreams usually refers to the dreamer's sense of self-worth. Dreams of running short of money, for instance, can come at times of change, when we question our own value.

> Just after my youngest child left home, I decided to take leave from work and go on a holiday on my own. My husband stayed at home. Every night during the first week I was away I dreamed either that my money had been stolen, or that I hadn't brought enough to pay my hotel bill.

This dreamer had suddenly found herself without the usual roles through which she found her self-esteem. For the moment, she was neither wife, mother, nor worker, and subconsciously feared that it was only through these roles that she was valuable. Losing her money, in the dream, reflects her fear of having lost her own sense of worth. Then later in the holiday, she had the following dream.

> I was getting some clothes out of my suitcase when I found a large wad of fifty dollar notes at the bottom. I didn't know how it had come to be there. I thought I must have put it in and forgotten about it. I was delighted.

The dreamer has found unexpected, hidden resources within herself: perhaps a surprising ability to enjoy her own company, or to make new friends, or perhaps pleasure in her new-found independence.

Sometimes money in dreams can refer to something else of value, such as love or time or energy.

Sometimes money in dreams can refer to something else of value such as love, time or energy.

> I dreamed my husband gave me counterfeit money for the housekeeping. I didn't say anything, but I felt puzzled and annoyed.

Money here probably refers to love. Somehow this dreamer is sensing that her husband's affection is not genuine at the moment and her subconscious mind is drawing her attention to this perception. The dream is inviting her to tell him how she feels, and find out what's going on with him.

MUD

We dream of mud, swamps or quicksand when we're feeling bogged down in life. Sometimes we may get stuck because we are wearing unsuitable shoes — in other words the roles and attitudes we have taken on are making it difficult for us to move on.

Sinking into the mud or quicksand is an indication of feeling overwhelmed. Struggling in quicksand — mentally wrestling with the problem, perhaps — only makes things worse. Often the best solution is to sit quietly, review our resources and allow the solution to come to us intuitively.

MUSIC

Music is an indication of 'atunement' or harmony with life. Discordant sounds reveal a sense of being out of tune with events or particular individuals who appear in the dream, while beautiful music represents a longing or a capacity for harmony with all of life. Such a dream can leave us with a feeling of great joy, as a oneness and flowing with life is one of humankind's deepest longings.

NUDITY

Appearing naked refers to the vulnerability we feel when stripped of our everyday roles — as in the intimacy of a close relationship, for example, where we reveal more about ourselves than usual.

Sometimes we might feel the same vulnerability in a work situation where we are staking a great deal on our performance and are anxious about the outcome — and dream of being naked in the workplace.

A dream of semi-nudity can refer to sexual vulnerability in particular.

> Just after I started college, I used to dream of going to lectures and realising when I got there that I was naked from the waist down. I felt excruciatingly ashamed and embarrassed, especially as there were men around, something I wasn't used to, having gone to an all-girls school.

The fact that the dreamer was partly clothed serves simply to emphasise her semi-nakedness. Such dreams are common in young people who are shy or vulnerable in relation to their sexuality and their bodies, and occur particularly from childhood to the early twenties. Reduced contact with the opposite sex probably increases these feelings, so as members of the opposite sex become more familiar and less scary, these dreams usually cease.

Dreaming of semi-nudity can refer to sexual vulnerability.

Sometimes an unpleasant sexual experience which leaves the individual angry or ashamed can also trigger off a dream of partial nudity.

NUMBERS

Numbers often appear in dreams — in the form of dates, a number of objects, time, age or an amount of money.

Numbers often appear in dreams, whether in the form of dates, a number of objects, time, age or an amount of money. They can be difficult to interpret, as the dream will often disguise the context.

> In my dream, I met a strange woman who told me that she had had two rich husbands and could now buy whatever she wanted.

In real life this dreamer had never married. However over the previous two years she had been extremely successful in her business and had acquired money and confidence. The two rich husbands of the dream represented the two previous years.

> I dreamed I went to a house where in the dream, though not in real life, I had once lived. The house number was very clear to me: twenty-five. It was rather poky and run-down and I was glad I had moved out.

Numbers can also refer to the age of a dreamer when a particular event occurred. When this dreamer was twenty-five, she was at a low ebb. As represented by the house, she was physically run-down and limited in her way of life. The dream shows her how she's changed since then.

Because numbers are so difficult to interpret, it's helpful to look at the rest of the dream first. In the above examples, understanding the symbolism of the rich husbands and the run-down house, respectively, set the context for understanding the numbers.

Usually, numbers have a personal meaning for the dreamer, referring to age, money or number of children for example. But they also have traditional significance and if we are unable to find a personal meaning, then the following may be helpful.

One
Union; doing something alone; independence; a fresh beginning; creativity.

Two
Partnership; finding a balance between conflicting demands; parenthood; putting other people before oneself; indecision.

Three
Friendship; family life; Trinity; harmony.

Four
Wholeness; completion; fulfilment; practical solution to a problem; work; service to others.

Five
Communication; freedom; adventure; curiosity; nature; human life; occasionally, conflict and disappointment.

Six
Harmony that comes from taking responsibility for one's life and actions; sex.

Seven
Sacredness; religion; solitude; meditation; the inner life.

Eight
Power; wealth; business.

Nine
Completion of a cycle; selflessness; pregnancy.

Ten
Wholeness; marriage; over-abundance.

Twelve
Months in the year; signs of the zodiac; disciples; often refers to time.

Twenty-four
Hours in the day.

Numerology is an ancient philosophy which makes use of numbers such as the date of birth to analyse character and predict the future. One of the techniques of numerology which can be used in dream interpretation is the adding together of the individual digits of a multi-digit number until a single figure is left for interpretation. For example, the individual digits of the number 563 are added thus: $5+6+3=14$, then the resulting 1 and 4 are added to produce 5, which is the number used in interpretation.

OBSTACLES
Anything that prevents the dreamer from reaching a destination in a dream, such as objects in the way, rough terrain to cover, or even rainy weather, represents the dreamer's perception of the obstacles to be overcome in achieving some goal.

> I dreamed I was going up to the top floor of a house. On the stairs were many items of furniture — chairs, tables, boxes, bookshelves — and I had to climb over them to get up. Eventually I got there, with much relief. Then I saw there was a lift, and I could have come up with no trouble at all.

'Upstairs' is this dreamer's destination, perhaps referring to achieving some new height in her career or creative activities. Yet many obstacles stand in her way and she needs to review what they are: other people? lack of time or self-discipline? competing demands? lack of confidence? The irony suggested by this dream is that it is actually unnecessary for her to surmount these obstacles — that somehow she is making a great deal of unnecessary work for herself by dealing with them when she can avoid them entirely and go straight to the top.

OCEANS

Oceans reflect the enormous power and depth of subconscious feelings.

> I dreamed I was on the beach watching the most enormous waves breaking on the shore — they must have been sixty feet high. I was terrified, thinking I was going to be swept away and drowned.

This dreamer is afraid of being overwhelmed by the enormity of her feelings. She may not even be conscious of what the feelings are, but has probably had some change in her life recently — perhaps in her work, her relationships or even her thinking about life — that has deeply stirred her. She's worried that if she really allows herself to contact her emotions they will 'sweep her away' and take her over, with dire consequences.

Yet intense emotion does not have to be acted out; if we feel intensely sexual towards someone who is not our regular partner, we don't have to make love with him or her to be aware of the feeling. If we are intensely angry with someone, we don't have to fly into a rage next time we see that person.

There is a third alternative between repressing feelings and acting them out, and that is to simply allow them to be there, to watch them and to accept them as part of our psychological landscape. Simply watching and accepting ourselves are the keys to self-understanding.

Furthermore, repressing emotions takes a large amount of psychological energy and can leave us feeling tired from the effort. Accepting our feelings can give us new vitality and energy.

This process is illustrated in the following dreams.

> I had three dreams about the sea, around the time I met my husband. In the first one I was at the beach, fully dressed and paddling in the shallows. I could see big waves further out, but said to myself — no way! I'll just lift my skirt up a bit and get my feet wet.
>
> Then a few weeks later I dreamed I was on a cliff watching the ocean, the waves pounding in — I didn't feel anything, just watched calmly.
>
> Then about two or three months later, I dreamed I was surfing. I don't surf in real life, and I was amazed at how enjoyable it was to just be carried by the momentum of the waves.

The big waves in the first dream probably represent the dreamer's feelings of love, and the fears of hurt and rejection that go with it. She was by no means ready to dive in yet.

Later, her dream shows her quietly watching and waiting, perhaps to see what develops.

And the third dream indicates that she has 'taken the plunge' and is allowing herself to be carried — though not carried away — by her feelings.

The same applies to all subconscious emotions, even the ones we think of as negative: awareness and acceptance allows them to be integrated into our everyday lives, bringing new energy and aliveness.

OPPOSITES

Dreams frequently compare opposites, asking us to consider the differences between the various aspects of ourselves, or a situation.

Dreams frequently compare opposites.

Up/Down

A dream which compares up and down is usually distinguishing between the mind with its socially conditioned ideas and beliefs about how things should be, and the instincts, which wish to pursue their goals regardless of convention.

> I went to a house in my dream. Upstairs there was a lecture going on, attended by a number of quite serious-looking people, while downstairs there was a party with lots of fun and dancing. I couldn't make up my mind which to go to.

This dreamer can't decide between the serious activities of the mind (the lecture upstairs) and having fun (the party downstairs).

In fact, no decision is required: in real life, and probably the dream, too, he can have both, by spending part of his time 'upstairs' and part 'downstairs'. Often we feel we must choose between the two, when it is quite possible to enjoy some of both.

Front/Back

'Front' usually refers to our conscious personality, which we like to project to the world, whilst 'back' refers to our hidden, subconscious aspects.

> I dreamed I had changed my hair colour. The front was dyed blond, but when I looked in a mirror, I noticed that the back was black.

This dreamer probably sees herself as having qualities associated with the colour white — freshness, niceness and purity. Yet there's another side to her, qualities which are probably still unconscious and undeveloped. Behind her light personality are hidden power, earthiness and passion. She probably keeps them hidden for fear that their expression would be socially unacceptable. Yet the dream shows that they do exist and is drawing them to her attention so that she can begin to bring them into her everyday life in a way that is acceptable to her.

Out/In

The outside refers to the 'front' we present to the world, while the inside refers to the 'inner' man or woman — the realm of feelings, dreams and private thoughts.

OUT/IN — See Opposites

PARALYSIS

If we both want and fear the same thing, we can find ourselves 'stuck' in a dream.

If we want and fear the same thing, particularly sexually, we can find ourselves 'stuck' in a dream; we want to move towards it and run away simultaneously and end up unable to move at all.

> I dreamed I was being chased by a man with a gun. I tried to run but the lower part of my body was paralysed and I could hardly move.

The gun is a phallic symbol, so this dreamer is being pursued by a man representing powerful sexual feelings. Part of her finds this terrifying and tries to flee, yet another part wants to encounter her sexuality and stays put. The result is a dream of being stuck or fixed to the spot or paralysed.

Once this inner split has become conscious, rather than buried in the dreamer's subconscious mind, the dream has served its purpose and will not recur. So how do we go about understanding and dealing with a conflict like this?

The first step is to identify the subject of the conflict. Usually it's a sexual matter, but occasionally it may concern work, school or family. The details of the dream will provide further clues to its precise meaning.

The fear is the strongest emotion in a dream of being chased, so the second step is to identify why we are afraid. If it's a sexual fear for instance, perhaps we are afraid of being overwhelmed by our desire; of our vulnerability; of the possible consequences of the sexual act; of acting against family or religious injunctions. Simply acknowledging our fears by writing down the details and facing them squarely is a major step in resolving the conflict.

Next, acknowledge the part that wants to stay put — in our example, the part that wants to experience sexual feelings. It may be harder to acknowledge than the fear, but the dream of being paralysed would not have occurred unless the desire was there, so it's important to find it and face it. Perhaps it is sexuality in general, perhaps it is desire for a partner who is unsuitable or unavailable. Writing down what we can about this side of the conflict is the next step.

Finally we take some *action* to resolve the conflict. For example, we review our moral code to see whether it is right for us, and if not, begin to explore other precepts for living. Or we review our list of fears to see how realistic they are — it may be that they are simply frightening fantasies. Or if these fears stem from ignorance, we might buy or borrow some books in order to read up on the matter.

Once the dream has been understood in detail, and some action taken to resolve the conflict, then the dreamer will be released.

PEOPLE

Most dreams are full of people, ranging from intimate friends and family, to long-forgotten acquaintances to total strangers.

Dreams about people can be difficult to interpret in that the characters frequently have a symbolic meaning which takes some persistence to decipher. Occasionally a dream character will stand for himself, but more often represents some aspect of our own personality.

Most dreams are full of people, ranging from intimate friends and family to total strangers.

Acquaintances or Friends From the Past

Acquaintances or friends from the past are usually chosen for a part in a dream because they symbolise an aspect of the dreamer, or something that's presently occurring in the dreamer's life. Sometimes the person's name is the only reason why he or she is in the dream, especially if the person is from the distant past.

> I dreamed about a girl from my old workplace, called Sue Johns, whom I haven't seen or thought of for twenty years. She had moved into my house and was in the process of unpacking all her clothes into my wardrobe.

This dreamer's husband was called John, and after some reflection, she realised that 'the Johns girl' was taking over her life — in other words, rather than making decisions on the basis of what she herself wanted, she was choosing what to do, what to cook, where to go, and especially what to wear, on the basis of what she thought would please him. In this dream, the old friend appeared only because of her name.

An acquaintance or old friend can be chosen as a 'stand-in' for someone who is important to us at present. Perhaps we are reluctant to face some unpalatable truth about this person: our subconscious mind then substitutes a person with a similar name, occupation or nationality, for example, to get the message across.

Finally, the dream character can represent some aspect of the dreamer, such as motherliness, passion, orderliness, love of freedom or even exhaustion! So if it's not clear why a person has appeared

A dream character often represents some aspect of the dreamer, such as motherliness, passion, or even exhaustion!

in the dream, then it's probably because of what we perceive as their dominant characteristic, which the subconscious mind sees as active in us at the moment.

Babies

A baby represents the birth of some creative project or potential in the individual, perhaps a new job or relationship which will bring out our hitherto latent talents or qualities.

The rest of the dream, such as the birth circumstances and role of the dreamer (as mother, midwife, observer, etc) should cast further light on the nature of these new developments.

Children

Children hardly ever represent their real-life selves in dreams, which is fortunate, as so many dreams about our children have them sick, lost or dying. Instead they stand for the childlike aspect of the dreamer: vulnerability, trust, spontaneity and playfulness. In our competitive society these qualities tend to be downgraded and suppressed, yet without them we cannot relate intimately to our partners, friends and families.

If we suppress these qualities in the interests of self-preservation, or making a career, or if we have hardened ourselves to cope with life's demands, then we may have the following kind of dream.

> I dreamed I went into a room in my house that I'd forgotten about, and found a little girl there. I was horrified, because I knew she was mine and I'd forgotten about her, too. She looked very neglected — thin, weak and sick — and I knew I'd have to do something urgently to get her better.

Often the child in the dream will be one of the dreamer's own children and the dreamer will wake in horror feeling that the child is in danger in real life. This is rarely the case. The child stands for the dreamer's own childlike qualities that are in danger of being lost.

Sometimes the dream will explain what is required in order for the childlike qualities to be redeemed.

> I dreamed that my six-year-old daughter had been staying with neighbours. When I went to collect her, she was sitting with them at a very elaborate dining table and looked very pale. She had to be on her best behaviour and join in the adult conversation. I thought: 'This is ridiculous! It's no way to expect a kid to behave'. I gave her a big hug and we went to the beach together.

This dreamer is just coming to the realisation that her inner child needs time to be playful and close to others rather than having these qualities suppressed to conform to other people's expectations. She needs hugs, and time to enjoy herself in a relaxed way.

Sometimes, of course, children in a dream do stand for themselves. If there is an important aspect of the relationship between the dreamer and child that the dreamer is unaware of, then the dream will point it out.

> I dreamed that I was going on holidays with my new husband. My three-year-old (from my previous marriage) was with us in the car, but after we had left, I realised that my six-year-old wasn't with us. I looked back and saw him running after the car, calling to us.

This dream suggests that the elder child has been 'left by the wayside' in the formation of the new family. Perhaps the dreamer's attention has been taken up with wedding plans or moving to a new home, and she has expected him to be more independent than he is able to be. The dream is showing her that she could be more sensitive to her son's needs.

Dead People

Dreams of the dead are very common. Sometimes they inspire fear, at other times, joy. Frequently, a recently dead relative will appear in a dream with a message for the dreamer: often that all is well, and not to worry.

Such dreams have been known since dream records were first kept thousands of years ago. Who knows where they come from? Perhaps they represent a genuine communication from the dead person; perhaps they are the subconscious mind's way of providing comfort to the dreamer when it is most needed.

Other dreams, far from being comforting, are worrying or frightening. Such dreams are most likely to occur when the relationship between the dreamer and the dead person has been left unresolved in some way, and can include dreams where the dead person 'warns' the dreamer that his turn will soon follow. Perhaps the dreamer felt guilty or angry or estranged from the dead person, or perhaps many things were left unsaid, even the depth of the dreamer's love. The dreams are an attempt to resolve these feelings.

The fact that one person in a relationship (whether it's that of parent/child, brother/sister, husband/wife, friends and so on) has died, does *not* mean that the opportunity to express feelings and previously unspoken thoughts has been lost.

Dreams of the dead have been known of since dream records were first kept thousands of years ago.

An extremely effective way to express these thoughts is to write a letter to the dead person explaining all these feelings and responses, without reservation. Often, emotions that have been too uncomfortable to feel, such as guilt towards the person, or resentment or need, will emerge and find expression on paper.

Don't hold anything back. After all the person won't actually receive the letter. Its purpose is to clarify all the pain and confusion of an unresolved relationship.

As a guide, write a paragraph (as long as you want) beginning: 'I'm angry with you because . . .'; a paragraph beginning: 'I'm sad and hurt with you because . . .'; another beginning: 'I'm afraid because . . .' and a fourth beginning: 'I love you because . . .'

This is not an easy process. Sometimes more than one letter will be required, over a period of several weeks, before we can forgive ourselves, and the dead person, and feel that all that can be, has been resolved.

If you wish, you can post the letter to some place where you think the dead person might be. Despite the old wounds that this process can temporarily reopen, its completion ensures that frightening dreams about the dead person will never occur again.

Family Members — See **Family**

Lover or Spouse

The dreamer's lover or spouse often appears in dreams. If he or she does not, then this is significant in itself, perhaps indicating that the relationship has become empty or unimportant.

The dreamer's partner frequently represents him or herself, with the dream revealing the present state of the relationship, or some aspect of it that has been hidden from the conscious mind.

> My boyfriend came to pick me up wearing a funny blue hat. I thought it looked silly and asked him to take it off, but he insisted on wearing it out and said he was very proud of it.

The dreamer's lover or spouse often appears in dreams. The fact that he or she does not is significant in itself.

Blue represents the intellect, the source of which is usually seen to be the head, so the blue hat represents the boyfriend's thoughts and opinions. The dreamer thinks that many of these views are silly; perhaps she would prefer him to be more in touch with his feelings and intuitions rather than being rational and reasonable when they are together. However her subconscious mind is showing her how proud he is of his intellect — maybe of his capacity for reasoned debate — and that he is unlikely to change.

Sometimes the dream can define the partner's role in the dreamer's life.

> I dreamed that my husband held my hand and we took off from the ground, flying right over the rooftops. Then I decided to see if I could do it on my own and let go of his hand. I immediately went into a spin, and landed with a crash.

When she's with her husband, this woman 'flies high' — perhaps meaning that she is happy, creative and generally satisfied. Yet the dream shows how dependent upon him she is for this happiness. Without him, she spins out and comes down to earth with a crash. The dream is suggesting to her that she learns to become more independent.

What does it mean when we dream of our partner having an affair with someone else?

What does it mean when we dream of our partner having an affair with someone else? Occasionally it can be true; the subconscious mind has intuited what's going on and tells us in a dream.

More often, however, the dream reflects our own insecurity and fear of loss in the relationship. Sometimes this can be triggered by a new hobby or interest taken up by our partner, or an extra workload which takes the partner's focus away from the relationship.

Religious Figures

A NUN refers to the introspective, service-oriented or celibate part of the dreamer, and is also associated with traditional values and morality. She may also represent the dreamer's sister or mother.

A MONK has a similar meaning to a nun, and may also represent the dreamer's brother.

A PRIEST represents traditional moral authority. He can also stand for the dreamer's father.

Royal Family

Members of the royal family usually symbolise the dreamer's own family.

Members of the royal family symbolise the dreamer's own family.

> I dreamed I went to the Palace for afternoon tea. The Queen was in a foul temper and snapped at everyone, so as soon as I could I went off with the Princess of Wales and the Duchess of York to another room where we drank cappucino and looked at photographs.

The queen in this dream probably represents the dreamer's own mother, who seems to be going through a difficult and temperamental period. The Princess and Duchess would symbolise the dreamer's sisters or sisters-in-law who seem to be quite cosmopolitan women (drinking cappucino) with whom she shares pleasant memories (the photographs).

Twins
Twins refer to two aspects of the same person.

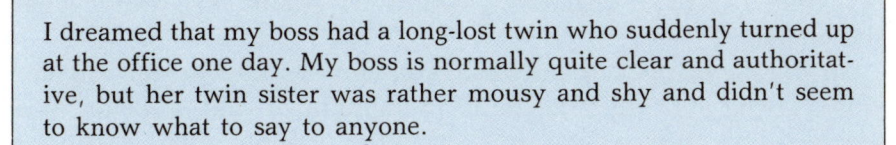

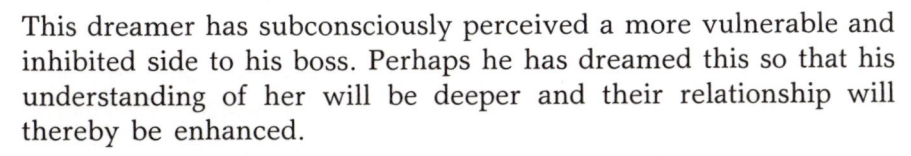

> I dreamed that my boss had a long-lost twin who suddenly turned up at the office one day. My boss is normally quite clear and authoritative, but her twin sister was rather mousy and shy and didn't seem to know what to say to anyone.

This dreamer has subconsciously perceived a more vulnerable and inhibited side to his boss. Perhaps he has dreamed this so that his understanding of her will be deeper and their relationship will thereby be enhanced.

Unknown Man
An unknown man in a woman's dream usually symbolises her so-called masculine characteristics: assertiveness, rationality, worldliness and power.

Women in our society have sometimes felt these qualities, particularly assertiveness and power, to be unacceptable and unfeminine, so many of us have 'disowned' them, pretending that the impulse to express them isn't there at all. Rather than going away, however, these impulses to be assertive and powerful gather strength, fester in the subconscious mind, and take their revenge on us for not expressing them by appearing in unpleasant dreams.

An unknown man in a woman's dream usually symbolises her more masculine characteristics, such as assertiveness, rationality, worldliness and power.

> I often dream that I'm being chased by a strange man. I don't know what he wants, perhaps to rape or attack me, maybe to kill me.

This dreamer's capacity to be sexually assertive, and to confront other people when necessary, has been suppressed. The suppression has caused them to grow stronger and become distorted so that they appear in her dream as threatened rape and physical assault, directed at the dreamer herself. These represent the dark side of assertiveness.

If she can develop the ability to ask for what she wants and to say 'no' to what she doesn't want — the positive side of assertiveness

— then the suppressed characteristics will become part of her conscious personality in their positive form and she will no longer have these frightening dreams. In fact, such dreams often disappear naturally as a women matures and becomes more sure of herself and her rights.

Of course, the unknown man in dreams isn't always frightening but can be supportive and caring. Sometimes he can appear as a woman dreamer's lover. Dreams like this indicate that the dreamer has integrated into her everyday life the qualities represented by the man and is able, for example, to stand her ground, and go for what she wants.

An unknown man in a woman's dream can also be seen as her guide to the subconscious mind. Sometimes a man appears in a dream simply to pass on a message to the dreamer about herself or her life.

> For some months I dreamed regularly of a red-headed man who was a thief. Sometimes he would try to break into my house (he was never violent or frightening), but more often he would take me out stealing with him or bring me a present of something he'd stolen.

An unknown man in a man's dream represents some unknown aspect of the dreamer himself.

This dreamer was very respectable in real life and insisted that her children always be scrupulously honest with her. This dream showed her another side to her character which she initially found very disturbing because it did not fit with her conscious picture of herself — she had the capacity to be dishonest herself. Her dishonesty took the most minor of everyday forms: a white lie here, a biro 'borrowed' from work there, but nevertheless revealed a side of her which had previously been hidden by her idealised self-concept.

When she accepted this side of herself, she was able to relax a little and accept this aspect of her children, too.

An unknown man in a man's dream represents some unknown aspect of the dreamer himself and parallels the appearance of an unknown woman in a woman's dream (see **Unknown Woman** below).

Unknown Woman

An unknown woman in a woman's dream represents some unknown aspect of the dreamer herself. Often this is negative and unflattering — a part of the dreamer which she rejects in herself and hopes that no-one else will notice. Having been rejected, this characteristic then recedes into the dreamer's subconscious mind, only to reappear in dreams, and often in an exaggerated form.

> A horrible woman was telling me how to run my life, bossing me about, pointing her finger, and generally being imperious and obnoxious. I tried to tell her that it was none of her business but she wouldn't listen.

This dreamer prides herself on her ability to let her family run their own lives and be independent. Yet the dream shows that there is another side to her which is authoritarian and controlling. It may appear in small ways with her family which she writes off as 'irritability' or 'pre-menstrual tension'; or it may have her as its focus so that she finds that she is excessively self-disciplined and controlled and won't allow herself to be spontaneous.

The key is to realise that she has this tendency, and notice when it is in action, usually at times of stress. Having accepted it as part of her personality she can then decide whether or not to allow it into her behaviour — when she is unaware of it, she has no control over it whatsoever.

Not all unknown women in dreams are negative. Sometimes unknown women of great beauty and wisdom can appear, representing the spiritual resources that we all have, but, in our culture, are not encouraged to acknowledge or use.

The unknown woman in a man's dream parallels the unknown man in a woman's dream. She represents the dreamer's 'feminine' qualities — nurturance and openness to feeling. Sometimes men dream of the 'inner woman' in a highly sexual way. This does not necessarily reflect on the quality of a man's sex life, but is the subconscious mind's most compelling way of drawing the man's attention to the need to develop his inner, feminine qualities.

Sometimes, a man's 'inner woman' can be terrible or grotesque.

The unknown woman in a man's dream represents his more 'feminine' qualities of nurturance and openness to feeling.

> I dreamed that an old hag came into my bedroom and woke me up. She was so ugly that I was afraid. She pointed her finger at me and told me all the things that were wrong with me and all the things I'd messed up.

Such dreams occur when a man has neglected his capacity for tender relationships; his feeling nature has turned ugly, bitter and critical. Any man's dream about an unknown woman is inviting him to experience and express his feelings of love and vulnerability.

Again, like the unknown man in a woman's dream, the unknown

woman in a man's dream can be a messenger from the subconscious. Other aspects of the dream will provide clues to its precise meaning.

Naturally, like any dream figure, her messages are not intended to be taken literally, but need to be interpreted carefully to decipher their meaning.

PINK — See Colours

PHOTOS — See Camera

PLACES

The setting of a dream is often quite clear to the dreamer even if he or she has never been there in real life, and even if it looks totally different in the dream. We *know* it's Hawaii or Egypt or the Gold Coast even if those places are unfamiliar to us.

When this happens, the location is an important clue to the meaning of the dream. Usually it has been included in the dream because it has particular associations for the dreamer — unlike other symbols, places do not seem to have a similar meaning for everyone.

> Over a few months I had repeated dreams about being at Coogee Beach — sometimes on the rocks, sometimes on the waterfront, sometimes in a nearby house. The content of each dream was quite different, except for the location.

This dreamer was baffled about the meaning of the dream setting until he recalled that many years before he had had a secret affair with a woman who lived at Coogee. The dreams he had which were set at Coogee were about aspects of himself and his life which he wished to keep secret from other people: Coogee symbolised the place in himself where things were kept hidden.

Our memories of a place are the best guide to its meaning.

The dreamer's memories of, or associations with, a place are the best guide to its meaning. America, for instance, might be exciting and full of opportunity to one dreamer, and brash and materialistic to another. India might be mysterious and colourful to one, and simply crowded and unhygienic to another.

Keeping records of dreams over an extended period — a year or more — shows that locations are often repeated, indicating that whatever they represent is a recurring theme in the life of the dreamer.

PRISONS

Prisons, of course, represent our feeling of being trapped. Usually we are trapped in a situation because of our own attitudes and fears: we stay in a stifling marriage because we are afraid of being alone; we stay in a well-paid but deadening job because we fear financial insecurity or simplifying our lifestyle.

Dreams of prison require careful thought. What is it that traps us? What is the price of freedom — facing my fear, guilt, loneliness etc? Am I willing to pay this price? Even if we decide to stay in our prison after analysing our situation, an honest analysis often shows us how much power to choose we actually have — that we stay in our stifling circumstances out of our fear or dependency, rather than because we must, or because we are victims of circumstance. Facing our fear, even if we take no action, is to step towards inner freedom.

Dreaming of someone else in prison can be the subconscious mind's perception of their entrapment; or alternatively the person can represent an aspect of ourselves that we do not allow ourselves to experience or express.

PROSTITUTES

Prostitutes in dreams have different meanings depending on the sex of the dreamer. In a woman's dream a prostitute usually represents the idea of selling any kind of service — not necessarily of a sexual nature.

> I dreamed I went to the office and discovered that I worked as a prostitute, not as a secretary. All the secretaries were in the same position, and the two pimps were our supervisor and the general manager.

In a woman's dream a prostitute usually represents the idea of selling any kind of service — not necessarily sexual.

This kind of dream is not uncommon, and reflects the dreamer's attitude to her work. Perhaps she feels she is treated as a commodity rather than as a person, and works in this office simply for the money, rather than for any kind of personal satisfaction. The supervisor and the general manager seem to be the ones she sees as responsible for the situation!

A man's dream about a prostitute is likely to have a more specifically sexual meaning. Perhaps it reflects his attitude to women generally as purchasable sexual objects. Or a dream that a particular woman is a prostitute may reveal a fear that he is receiving her sexual favours not from love but from a desire for material gain.

A man's dream about a prostitute is likely to have a more specifically sexual meaning.

PURPLE — See Colours

RAIN — See **Weather**

RED — See **Colours**

RELIGIOUS FIGURES — See **People**

RIVERS

Rivers represent the movement of life — the current underlying our progress from birth to death.

Rivers represent the movement of life — the current underlying our progress from birth to death.

> I dreamed I was on a rafting trip down the river. It had been raining heavily and the water was quite high. I knew there were rapids ahead and I decided to have a swim in a lovely waterhole before I took on the white water.

The heavy rain indicates that this dreamer has a lot of energy for change — the high water sweeps away stagnant pools. She is aware that there is excitement and perhaps danger ahead — perhaps a move, or change of job or lifestyle — and she is taking the opportunity to gather energy in a quiet moment before she takes on the challenge.

> I was standing on the banks of a river and could see my daughter, who was crying, on the other side. I had to go across and get her, but I felt very frightened, as the water was deep and murky and fast.

Across the river is something very precious to the dreamer — her vulnerable, playful, spontaneous qualities as represented by her daughter (see **Children**, page 91). She knows she must bring these qualities back into her life, but is afraid of what is required to do this — traversing the deep and murky waters. Perhaps these represent her fears of other people's disapproval if she allows herself to have fun and express her feelings, or her fears of being hurt if she shows her vulnerability. In other words she fears the price she may have to pay for immersing herself in the 'waters' of life — for being fully alive.

ROADS

Roads reveal the present state of the dreamer's 'life path'. A freeway suggests that the way is open for rapid movement towards one's destination, whilst a bumpy road shows that the dreamer's progress could be much smoother!

A side-track speaks for itself, and taking the wrong road, or getting lost, shows that there is an area of our lives where we have lost our way. The details of the dream may tell us which area this is. Perhaps we are lost with our lover or spouse, indicating that the relationship is 'on the wrong track', or perhaps we get lost on the way to work, or even in our workplace, suggesting that it's the wrong job for us, or that we simply feel 'lost' there.

RUBBISH

Clearing or sorting out old junk and rubbish represents the process of eliminating what we don't need in our lives any more.

> In my dream I went down to the cellar of my grandmother's house to have a clean-up. I thought there was valuable stuff there, but it was full of rubbish. I packed most of it into garbage bags ready to throw out, and felt very satisfied.

The dreamer's life will tell her what the rubbish symbolises. She may be 'cleaning up' a relationship, simplifying her lifestyle, or even changing her diet from 'junk' food to natural, wholesome products, and thereby cleaning up her body. The action of the dream probably takes place in her grandmother's house because she is taking a new direction and clearing out the old.

SCHOOL

School is a place of learning and so for adults, usually represents the 'school of life'. Perhaps some important life lesson is being learned, and the details of the dream will provide further information about what it is.

For other people, school can represent limitations to freedom, and arbitrary rules.

> I dreamed I was back at school. The teacher told us we were going to play Bingo, and I asked if I could go to the library instead. He said no. Then I thought: this is ridiculous! I'm thirty-six years old and I can do as I please! I walked out, and no-one said anything or tried to stop me.

For some people, school can represent limitations to freedom, and arbitrary rules.

The dreamer was imposing rules upon herself — behaving in a way that she thought she should — which prevented her from doing what she wanted to. Around the time of this dream she realised that her self-imposed rules (e.g. not going out by herself at night to an art class she wanted to attend; doing all the housework herself instead of getting the family to do their share) were limiting her enjoyment of life, and that freeing herself from them would have only beneficial consequences.

SEEDS

The seed of an idea or of personal development may be represented in a dream by sowing or planting.

Seeds refer to the earliest potential for new growth. The seed of an idea, of a relationship or development within the individual, may be represented in a dream by sowing or planting.

> When my youngest son started school, I started thinking about getting a job. I had a dream where I went to work in a plant nursery. I was sorting out seeds, deciding which ones to plant, which ones would grow best. Does this mean I should get a job in a nursery?

Usually, dreams don't intend to be taken literally. This dreamer should get a job in a nursery if it interests her sufficiently, but the dream has a deeper meaning. It is suggesting that she sorts through her ideas about what she might do, to work out what will suit her best and what will provide the best opportunity to develop her potential.

SEX

Almost everyone dreams about sex at some point in life.

Almost everyone dreams about sex at some point in life. Dreams ranging from kissing and cuddling to intercourse are quite normal.

Sometimes we dream of making love with our usual partner, in which case the dream is probably reaffirming our love and desire for that person, but quite often we dream of making love with someone else entirely.

Sometimes such dreams are pointing out a previously ignored sexual attraction to the person, but more often dream partners are selected for symbolic reasons — for what they *represent* rather than who they *are* in real life.

> I have been with my present boyfriend for more than two years now, but lately I have been dreaming of having sex with my previous boyfriend, who I haven't seen for about three years. I find these dreams very upsetting, as I love my boyfriend very much and don't want to make love with anyone else.

This dream doesn't indicate that the dreamer wants to go back to her previous lover — it's clear that she is happy in her present relationship.

The previous boyfriend represents some quality or way of being that the dreamer wishes to be 'united' with — something she wants to express in her own life. What was the earlier lover like? Was he creative? Practical? Sexy? Talkative? Conventional? Witty? Whatever qualities first come to mind when the dreamer thinks of him are probably the characteristics that she would like to develop in herself. When she identifies what they are and begins to express them, she will no longer have dreams of making love to her ex-boyfriend.

The dreams may also indicate that in some respects she wishes that her present boyfriend was more like the other man — perhaps he was a more tender lover, or less moody, or more generous, for instance.

The same principles apply to any dreams of making love with an unexpected partner, including actors, singers and other well-known people who are not personally known to the dreamer.

Now and again, very sensitive dreamers can dream of making love with someone who they don't find particularly attractive, but who is attracted to them. Perhaps they have picked up at a subliminal level that the person finds them desirable, and the dream is seeking to make them conscious of that fact.

Incest

Dreaming of making love with a member of one's own family can leave the dreamer feeling distressed and ashamed. However, such dreams do not necessarily reveal a wish for sex with the person, but

Dreams of making love with a family member do not necessarily reveal a wish for sex. It is more likely such dreams represent a wish for love.

should be taken symbolically — they represent a wish for love. They indicate that we want to get closer to that person, to love and be loved by him or her, rather than to *make* love. Sex is usually symbolic of love in these dreams, rather than a literal desire.

Homosexuality

Psychologists believe that we are all, to some extent, attracted to members of our own sex, even if we never consciously think about it, and never act it out.

So dreams about sex with members of our own gender simply bring to our attention that part of ourselves which is drawn to the love of our own sex. They don't necessarily mean we are homosexual — it is a normal part of being human to feel, or dream about, this kind of attraction.

SHAPES

Shapes can refer to what shape we're in, or what shape our lives are taking.

Shapes can refer to what shape we're in, or what shape our lives are taking.

Sometimes the shape will be undefined, suggesting that we are not sure where we are or where to go next. If we ask ourselves: 'What does this shape remind me of?' and allow it to develop in our imagination, then we may receive further information which will allow the future to take shape in our thoughts.

More often, however, shapes will be distinctly defined. Here are some of the meanings traditionally assigned to different shapes.

Circles and Circular Objects

Circles and circular objects represent wholeness and completion, harmony and balance.

> I dreamed I was about to open a restaurant and went into the building to arrange the tables. They were all round! A whole restaurant full of round tables! This was at a time when I had left my old job and was about to start work as a counsellor.

The round tables which made such an impression on this dreamer represent a confirmation of her new choice of career, indicating that it is likely to bring her a sense of completion and satisfaction. The symbol of the restaurant is a nice touch, too, suggesting that she sees her role as the emotional 'nourisher' of her clients.

Crescent

A crescent, such as a new or old moon, is a symbol of the power of the feminine, with its capacity for feeling and intuition.

Sometimes it will appear in a woman's dream when she is developing confidence in her strength as a woman and her capacity to understand and express herself creatively. It can also appear when the dreamer's life has been emotionally barren, presaging a new emphasis on feeling rather than thinking or action.

Cross
A cross, with the four arms pointing in different directions, often indicates inner conflict, as the dreamer feels the pull of four different and seemingly irreconcilable needs or demands. However, according to tradition, it is through the pain of feeling 'torn apart' and reaching some resolution of the opposites, that the individual develops to full potential.

Squares and Square Objects
Squares and square objects refer to the bringing into being of creative ideas, and to the materialising of plans and intentions.

Stars
Stars represent the inner knowing which guides us towards our destiny in life, and in a dream, invites us to trust our intuition.

Triangles
Triangles occasionally represent the three aspects of mankind — the body, mind and spirit — but more often relate to the dreamer's sex life. The triangle is an ancient symbol of female genitals.

SHOES
Shoes refer to our situation in life. The expression 'I'd like to be in his shoes' indicates a wish for another person's opportunity, riches or beautiful lover, and likewise, our own shoes represent our own circumstances.

Changing our shoes may symbolise changing our circumstances; getting them wet may suggest that our present situation is such that we are becoming over-emotional (water representing the emotions); losing our shoes or having them stolen may reveal that we are allowing ourselves to be victims of circumstance in some unnecessary way; cleaning them indicates cleaning up our lives.

Shoes can also have a similar meaning to feet in that they connect us with the ground, or reality, and are our means of taking steps in our lives.

SHOWERS
Showers refer to our everyday, routine communications with the subconscious mind, in noting our dreams for example, or paying attention to our moods and feelings.

> I dreamed I was having a shower with my bathing cap, slacks and blouse on. This was at a time when I had been extremely busy looking after my grandchildren whilst my daughter was in hospital having her third child.

This dreamer is probably quite attuned to her subconscious mind. She may be at a time in her life when she can sit quietly and reflect on her relationships, pleasures, plans and dreams. So when a busy time interrupts her everyday, quiet communion with herself, the subconscious mind can't get through to bathe her with its waters, and sends her a dream about it.

SNAKES — See Animals

SNOW — See Weather

SOLDIERS

Soldiers can represent discipline, control and regimentation.

Soldiers and the armed forces generally can either be a part of an inner conflict, or a conflict with someone else.

However, they can also represent discipline, control and regimentation, perhaps reflecting some aspect of the dreamer's life: relationships, work or attitude to domestic life for instance.

SPACE

Outer space is often a symbol for 'inner space' and suggests the limitless dimensions of our own being.

Spaceships are our symbolic vehicles for exploring these inner dimensions — dream interpretation, for example, is one way of looking within and so may itself be represented in a dream as a spaceship.

Aliens, as the inhabitants of space, may symbolise strange parts of ourselves — aspects that we are only just encountering and coming to know. Sometimes they can be terrifying, at other times the bearers of wisdom from the outermost limits of ourselves.

Aliens can sometimes refer to a sense of 'alienation'. If the alien of our dreams is walking the earth lonely and sad and longing for home, then perhaps this is our experience of life at the moment — yearning to feel part of a world that seems strange and foreign and to feel connected with other people.

A dream like this is showing us that we must reach out to other people emotionally, learn the skills needed to fit into our environment, and do whatever else is required to feel at home with ourselves.

SPIDERS — See **Animals**

SPOUSE — See **People**

SQUARE — See **Shapes**

STARS — See **Shapes**

STORMS — See **Weather**

SUNSHINE — See **Weather**

SWIMMING

Swimming involves immersion in water — the realm of the subconscious and feelings. Often, because it is a physical activity, it can refer to sex. Whatever it refers to, the circumstances are a metaphor for our experience: are we struggling against the current — in other words, battling against our emotions and sexual impulses? Is it a sensual, enjoyable swim in balmy waters? If so we are presently at home and comfortable with our feelings. Is there a danger of drowning? We may fear being overwhelmed by intense feelings, perhaps of anger, sadness, vulnerability or sexuality.

TELEPHONE

The telephone is a means of getting in touch with other people and communicating with them. Who are we phoning in the dream? And what do we want to say?

Dreams about telephones often involve difficulties in 'getting through' such as forgetting the number, being unable to dial, or being disconnected. These indicate problems in communication with the person we want to contact. In real life, we need to be clear about what we want to put across, why, and to whom, and be willing to persist until the message has been heard and understood.

Occasionally, an important message will be delivered to the dreamer from the subconscious mind via a dream telephone. Which part of the personality is it coming from — the inner child? A smooth operator? A wise man or woman? The message should be carefully considered, as it may contain helpful advice.

Occasionally, an important message will be delivered from the subconscious mind via a dream telephone.

THEATRE

The 'theatre of life' is often represented in dreams by the stage, plays and actors. What's happening on stage reflects what's happening in the dreamer's life, or what she fears will happen.

The 'theatre of life' is often represented in dreams by the stage, plays and actors.

> I dreamed I was in a play put on by a local drama group. But when I went on stage, the play was unfamiliar to me. I didn't know what to do, and couldn't remember any lines.

Assuming that the play is a metaphor for this dreamer's life, she is feeling insecure and lacking in confidence in playing her part in the world. Perhaps she feels awkward socially and often doesn't know what to do or say. An assertiveness or confidence training course could help her overcome her shyness.

If the dreamer suddenly finds she must improvise her lines, then the subconscious mind might be inviting her to lighten up and become more spontaneous rather than operating from a rigid script or inflexible role.

TOILET

Going to the toilet is about eliminating what is no longer needed.

> In my dream I had to go to the toilet, but the only one available was out in the open air in full view of passers-by. I used it, feeling deeply embarrassed, but no-one seemed to notice or care.

This kind of dream is quite common. The dreamer is getting rid of something she no longer needs, such as old inhibitions or self-imposed limitations, but is afraid that other people will judge her for it. Yet her shame is unnecessary — the people in her life barely even notice, let alone condemn her.

Sometimes, of course, a dream of going to the toilet can simply indicate that the dreamer has a full bladder.

TRAINS

Trains represent our movement through life. Our dream behaviour reveals our progress on the way.

> I was on a train going north with my parents and a friend. My friend was going all the way to Queensland and I would have liked to go too, but instead I got off half-way with my parents and checked into an old-fashioned hotel.

The dreamer's friend represents the part of her that is adventurous and likes to go all the way with her experiences. However the dreamer is choosing another, more conservative way of being at the moment, where she goes along with her parents, representing, like the hotel, traditional values. This dream is reminding her that she does have a choice in her values and her actions.

Missing the train (or bus) in a dream indicates a fear of missing an opportunity, or fear of failing to achieve one's goals, particularly in one's career. Sometimes this can occur because the dreamer's goals have been set too high — or perhaps because she is tired and run down and simply doesn't have the energy to pursue them at a fast enough pace.

TREES

Trees represent our development in life. The roots show us both how we perceive our origins and how well connected we are to the earth of everyday reality, while the overall growth of the tree is an indication of our own characteristics. Perhaps it is strong and straight, or twisted and crooked in some way. Perhaps it soars towards the heavens, representing spiritual strength, or is old and gnarled, referring to the wisdom of age.

Trees represent our development in life.

Different trees can have their own meanings. A WEEPING WILLOW, for example, may represent our hidden sadness. An OAK TREE is traditionally a symbol of strength. An APPLE TREE was the Tree of Knowledge in the Garden of Eden, and so may refer to forbidden fruit.

TRIANGLES — See **Shapes**

TWINS — See **People**

UP/DOWN — See **Opposites**

VICTIM

In dreams, the dreamer is often a victim.

In dreams, the dreamer is often a victim. One may be the victim of a robbery, an assault or circumstances generally.

The dreamer is responsible, however, at a deep level, for creating the entire dream, complete with plot and cast. In some way then, we deliberately cast ourselves in the role of the powerless victim.

Why would we do such a thing? I believe we do this at a subconscious level, to draw our conscious attention to the ways in which we avoid responsibility in everyday life. Perhaps we allow ourselves to be used by friends and family, instead of coming out with a firm 'no' to their excessive demands. Perhaps we allow others to exploit us sexually, or at work, because we believe that this is the only way we will be accepted. Is acceptance worth it at this price?

Or perhaps we avoid responsibility for looking after ourselves by taking refuge in emotional or physical weakness. There are certain advantages to playing the role of victim or weak one — the dream, however, will often point out the disadvantages and encourage us to develop our disowned strength and responsibility for our lives.

VOLCANOES

Volcanoes refer to an eruption of inner fire or passion — perhaps sexuality or anger. The explosion usually occurs because these intense feelings have been suppressed for fear of the consequences of expressing them.

However, it is when they are first suppressed, and then later expressed with volcanic heat and explosion, that the consequences are a problem. Rather than acting out suppressed passions with outbursts of rage against others, or compulsive sexuality, other methods can be used to release these feelings, such as primal therapy or even an hour's writing every day to clarify and express emotions. Volcanic outbursts of feelings are often destructive.

WAR

Dreams about war refer to either inner conflict, or conflict with another person.

> When I was breaking up with my husband, I dreamed we were in a war zone — it was in Chile. A helicopter dropped bombs on us and we ran to escape it.

This dreamer confirmed the amount of hostility between herself and her husband — they were indeed 'in the wars': He had 'dropped a bombshell' on her about having had an affair with another woman, and things between them were very 'chilly'.

WATER

Water in dreams represents the subconscious mind. The subconscious mind holds many aspects of who we are that are more or less mysterious to us. Impulses that seem to come from nowhere, but which we 'must' follow — perhaps to speak in the heat of the moment, perhaps to act in an unexpected and spontaneous way — have their roots there. Behaviour that surprises even us is motivated from this deep place. And here too are stored feelings that are too painful or frightening for us to experience consciously — such as intense sexuality, rage, sadness, fear or vulnerability, and even love and passion.

All of these aspects of us, particularly our feelings, can be represented by water.

Water in dreams represents the subconscious mind.

WEATHER

Bright Sunshine

Bright sunshine refers to the light of conscious awareness. If the sunshine is a prominent feature of the dream it indicates that some 'illumination' of whatever it is casting its light on, is taking place.

Sometimes it can also appear as an indication of an end to emotional turmoil, particularly if it follows storms or cloudy weather or a struggle of some kind in the dream.

Heatwave

A heatwave in a dream is often a response to the dreamer's being overheated while asleep. If it's not caused by too many blankets, then it represents a sustained period of emotional heat in the dreamer's life — perhaps of intense sexuality or anger.

Lightning

Lightning represents the sudden flash of illumination, or bolt from the blue. Often a dream of lightning occurs a day or two before a major insight into oneself or one's life, or precedes an unexpected, spontaneous and far-reaching decision. It is as if the idea or insight is gathering 'energy' in the subconscious mind before it comes to conscious awareness, and the dream is an advance warning.

Rain
Rain usually represents relief from an emotional or intellectual drought — perhaps a new friendship or interest.

It can also refer to tears. If the dreamer is sad, but finds it difficult to cry, then the weather in the dream will do the weeping for her.

Snow
Snow represents emotional coldness or numbness.

> Soon after I was promoted in my job (I'd worked very hard for it), I dreamed I had reached the top of a mountain after a long climb. The view was good, but the summit was very cold and covered with a blanket of snow.

This dreamer has realised the peak of his present ambitions after a difficult haul and is pleased with the rewards (the view), but the cost has been the neglect of his emotional life, and the dream is pointing to his coldness and lack of feeling. It's important that he devote more time to personal relationships and allows himself to thaw out.

Storms

Storms refer to stormy weather in the dreamer's life.

Storms refer to stormy weather in the life of the dreamer — perhaps a severe inner conflict, perhaps conflict with a partner or spouse, or in the workplace. The dream may also indicate where shelter is to be found, or how the conflict can be resolved.

WHITE — See Colours

WILD ANIMALS — See Animals

YELLOW — See Colours